KNOCKOUT KNITS

NEW TRICKS FOR SCARVES, HATS, JEWELRY, AND OTHER ACCESSORIES

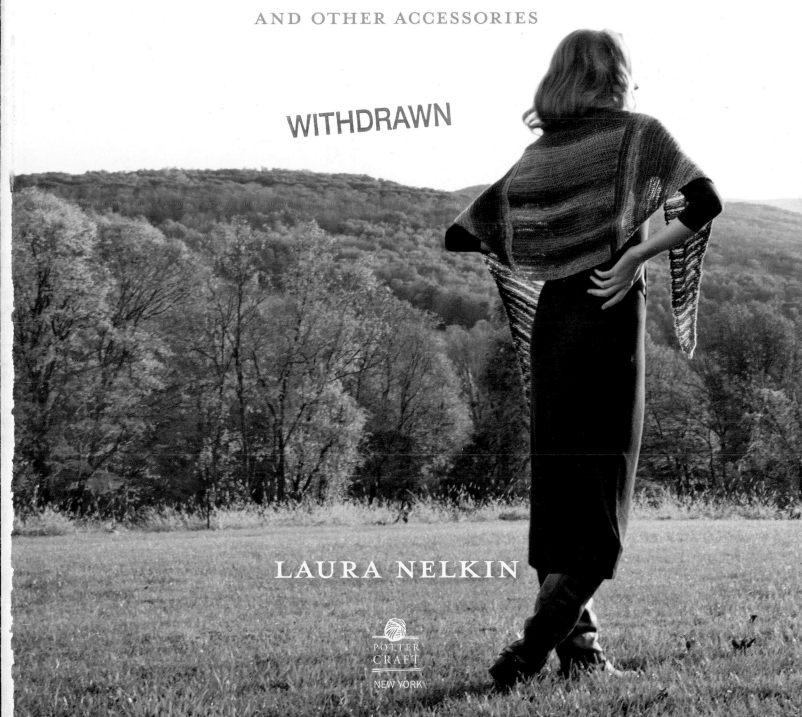

LAURA NELKIN

POTTER CRAFT

NEW YORK

*to my Ravelry group, for your knitting passion,
desire to learn, and heartfelt humor*

Published in the United States by Potter Craft, an
imprint of the Crown Publishing Group, a division
of Random House LLC, a Penguin Random House
Company, New York.

www.crownpublishing.com
www.pottercraft.com

POTTER CRAFT and colophon are registered
trademarks of Random House LLC.

Library of Congress Cataloging-in-Publication Data
Nelkin, Laura.
Knockout Knits / by Laura Nelkin.
— First edition.
pages cm
Includes bibliographical references and index.
1. Knitting—Patterns. I. Title.
TT825.N366 2013
746.43'2—dc23
2013038706

ISBN 978-0-385-34578-1
eBook ISBN 978-0-385-34579-8

Printed in China

Text and cover design by
La Tricia Watford
Photographs by Lauren Volo
Cover photographs by Lauren Volo

The author and publisher would like to thank the
Craft Yarn Council of America
for providing the yarn weight standards and
accompanying icons used in this book. For more
information, please visit www.YarnStandards.com.

10 9 8 7 6 5 4 3 2 1

First Edition

contents

introduction

I am obsessed with innovative knitting techniques and I adore playing with stitch patterns and constructions that explore the mechanics of knitting. This passion sparked the idea for this book of small knits. My hope is that I can help you stretch your knitting repertoire with these novel skills! Whether it's making a bead-embellished necklace for your best friend or a complex lace shawl just for you, the end result will make you smile and feel proud, of all that you've learned as well as of what you made. These are projects to knit as gifts, keep for yourself, or stockpile for the perfect occasion—such as Laxo Hat for a chilly ferry ride, Halli Shawl to throw over your shoulders at a formal event, or Quadro Convertible Shrug, your new favorite lace cover-up.

Over the course of three chapters, I'll share my favorite techniques: creating wrapped stitches, advancing lace skills, and knitting with beads. Each section begins with an introduction explaining the technique, why I love it, and why I think you will, too! I'll teach you the basic skills you need to know with step-by-step visuals before delving into the patterns. Within each chapter, the early patterns are relatively simple, always starting with a cuff as my teaching tool, and then they become progressively more complex. If you're like me, you seek a challenge and want to push the limits of what yarn and needles can do! You might find that you aren't interested in the first simple pattern, especially if you've already mastered that technique. It is perfectly fine to skip ahead to a design you love—you can always backtrack, if necessary, to hone a skill.

Consider yourself warned: By knitting the designs in this book, you are embarking on a potentially addictive—and definitely creative—journey!

NOTES ON YARN AND GAUGE

Once you decide on a pattern to follow, before you even cast on, you need to choose your yarn. There are many yarns on the market to pick from and I offer the following information to help you make a good decision.

Yarn

Choosing yarn is one of my favorite parts of designing and knitting. Huge decisions are made about the final piece at this critical first step. Fiber content, weight, and color all come into play. For this book, I picked out yarns that complemented the designs, but don't limit yourself to my choices. Your local yarn store (LYS) offers lots of options! Substitutions are easy but before you substitute another yarn for the one I suggest, make sure you consider the information in this section. You'll find more information on choosing appropriate yarn for knitting with beads on page 90, as you must consider the fiber's durability and construction.

Color

Glancing through the book, you will notice many hand-dyed yarns, both tonal and variegated. Commercially dyed yarns can sometimes seem flat by comparison, so I tend to gravitate toward hand-dyes. On larger pieces the subtly solid tonals definitely help a design come to life.

Wildly variegated yarns can obscure some stitch patterns; there's just no point spending hours on intricate stitches if no one can see them. The squint test (page 9) or a stitch pattern that plays well with several colors can help you skirt this dilemma. A number of my projects, such as the Reversible Undulating Waves Scarf and the Traversus Socks, work wonderfully with playful variegated yarns. For gradient yarns that have long color repeats, I designed the Halli Shawl, the Juego Cowl, and the Las Cruces Shawl, all of which showcase shifts in color without hiding your hard work.

Most of us (myself included) love to wear black, but knitting with it can be an awful drag without adequate lighting. It's easier on the eyes to knit with lighter- or brighter-color yarns, which also help stitch patterns show up better.

Fiber Content

When shopping for yarn, think about the fiber content of the yarn used in the sample. Fiber can drastically alter the look and feel of a design. For example, I selected an alpaca/silk blend with a fair amount of drape for the Quadro Convertible Shrug (page 67). Substituting a 100 percent wool yarn would create a stiff fabric that wouldn't fall as beautifully at the sleeve. Conversely, the Prolix Mitts (page 19) need a wool yarn with some structure. Pure cashmere yarn would feel sublime, but the mitts wouldn't stay up on your arm and they would pill the first time you wore them. I encourage you to experiment with lots of different fibers, but consider why the type of fiber used in the sample suits that design.

Weight

In each pattern, I list the yarn used by its weight. Take a look at the CYCA Standard Yarn Chart (opposite). It's a system of measuring weight and gauge that will better help you understand how to evaluate my choice.

I have a penchant for light fingering-weight yarn, known as three-ply yarn in the UK and Australia. Between lace- and sock-weight yarn, it's perfect for scarves and shawls—light and airy, but still substantial!

Gauge

If you are familiar at all with my workshops or patterns, you'll know that I am passionate about gauge and the necessity of working gauge swatches. Knitting patterns contain essential information in the gauge section—which is not necessarily the same as the gauge listed on the yarn's ball band. The pattern's gauge may be looser or tighter than the yarn manufacturer's gauge, because the designer wants the finished fabric to drape (or perform) in a specific way. For example, in the Folly Cloche (page 23), the gauge is denser than usual so that the hat has structure; if your fabric is too loose, the hat won't fit correctly. You may also knit more loosely (or tightly) and need to adjust your needle size to achieve the pattern's gauge.

All the specified gauge measurements are given based on blocked swatches. Wondering why this is? Gauge can shift after blocking, thanks to fiber content and styles of knitting. A cotton yarn knit on the same size needles as a wool yarn might have the

STANDARD YARN WEIGHT SYSTEM

CYCA	0 LACE	1 SUPER FINE	2 FINE	3 LIGHT	4 MEDIUM	5 BULKY	6 SUPER BULKY
Type of Yarns in Category	Fingering, 10-count crochet thread	Sock, Fingering, Baby	Sport, Baby	DK, Light Worsted	Worsted, Afghan, Aran	Chunky, Craft, Rug	Bulky, Roving
Knit Gauge Range* in Stockinette Stitch to 4" (10cm)	33–40 sts †	27–32 sts	23–26 sts	21–24 sts	16–20 sts	12–15 sts	6–11 sts
Recommended Needle in US Size Range	000–1	1–3	3–5	5–7	7–9	9–11	11 and larger
Recommended Needle in Metric Size Range	1.5–2.25mm	2.25–3.25mm	3.25–3.75mm	3.75–4.5mm	4.5–5.5mm	5.5–8mm	8mm and larger

* *Guidelines only:* The above information reflects the most commonly used gauges and needle sizes for specific yarn categories.

† Laceweight yarns are usually knitted on larger needles to create lacy, openwork patterns. Accordingly, a gauge range is difficult to determine. Always follow the gauge stated in the pattern.

same gauge preblocking, but those fibers will behave differently in the blocking process. It only takes an extra second to block a gauge swatch, and it's worth ensuring that your final knit will fit and that you have enough yarn.

That said, the more knitting experience you gain (which, for me, is directly related to how many knitting failures I've had), the more likely it is that you'll know when you can "get away" with shifting the gauge called for in a pattern. It is possible, but proceed with caution!

Yarn Weight Substitution
If you want to knit the Loco Shawl (page 77), but would rather stab your eyes out than knit it in a laceweight yarn, you can substitute a fingering-weight yarn. (Note that this does not apply to fitted items, which are beyond the scope of this book.) All you have to do is get the exact same gauge, blocked. Go up a needle size to test-knit a matching gauge swatch! Keep the following rules in mind:

• Gauge is measured over stitches and rows.

• As a typical rule, match stitch gauge first and row gauge second. For the designs in this book, stitch gauge is more important than row gauge.

• A looser gauge has *fewer* stitches per inch.

• A tighter gauge has *more* stitches per inch.

How to Knit a Gauge Swatch
Cast on 10 more stitches than the pattern gauge calls for and work for 10 rows more. If the gauge is given in rounds instead of rows, work your gauge swatch in the round.

Say the gauge listed on a pattern is 20 stitches and 28 rows = 4" (10cm) in stockinette stitch, blocked. First, cast on 30 stitches. Work in the pattern listed (in this case stockinette stitch) for 38 rows. Then bind off and block.

How to Block a Swatch

Once the swatch is knit, it is time to block it! Fill a small bowl or sink with warm water. Be careful that this water isn't too hot or too cold, either of which might shock the fibers, causing them to felt. Add some gentle soap or wool wash. Then place your swatch into the water and thoroughly wet all the fibers. Don't agitate it, but simply squeeze the swatch a bit. Then remove the swatch and roll it up in a towel to remove the extra moisture. Finally, lay this swatch flat, but *do not* stretch it out; the fibers should just be relaxed. Wool and wool blends can be measured wet, but if you are working with cotton, silk, or linen, wait until the swatch is dry, since those fibers can shrink a bit. If you are swatching a lace stitch, you will want to stretch out the swatch to simulate blocking the final piece; this is necessary to "open up" the lace stitches.

How to Measure and Adjust a Swatch

I always use an ironing board as a work surface and a ruler or measuring tape. With the swatch lying flat, measure the number of stitches over 4" (10cm). Repeat for the row gauge. Remember that stitches run horizontally and rows run vertically.

If you have too few stitches per inch (i.e., the gauge is loose), go *down* a needle size. This will tighten up the gauge by creating more stitches per inch.

If you have too many stitches per inch (i.e., the gauge is tight), go *up* a needle size. This will loosen up the gauge by creating fewer stitches per inch.

How to Check Gauge in Progress

Sometimes I want to see exactly how my piece is looking and fitting before it's finished. Especially with lace, it's hard to imagine the final fabric. I've been known to place all my stitches onto a lifeline (page 49) and block mid-knit to get an idea of how the design looks. If you are ever in doubt, take the time to do this! It's quite fun, and may inspire you to keep knitting.

SQUINT TEST

>> I always do this when choosing yarn. Hold the skein or ball at arm's length and squint at it. If one color stands out, that color will most likely be prevalent in the knitted fabric. Sometimes this is desirable, such as in a simple garter stitch knit, but oftentimes it leads to a project's disharmony as that one color will have a tendency to pop out and distract from the design.

wrapped STITCHES *at* PLAY

My favorite way to design is to play. In this chapter I show you creative techniques I've developed by playing with a simple stitch and manipulating it with extra wraps. If you are relatively new to knitting, this is the ideal chapter for us to begin exploring the craft together.

By wrapping the yarn more than once around your needle you create an elongated stitch, opening up a world of design possibilities. Elongated stitches can travel a longer distance without puckering the fabric, which allows for unexpected cabling and texture techniques. In the Laxo Hat (page 27), for example, the elongated stitches are crossed in a pattern, creating a "faux" cable stitch that works perfectly with hand-dyed yarn. In the Bootsy Boot Toppers (page 31), the elongated stitches are crossed in multiples so that the stitch pattern resembles a woven fabric. The Folly Cloche (page 23) utilizes another trick in which the elongated stitches are twisted 360 degrees on the needle, creating a traveling "cord" of stitches. I stumbled across this possibility when my double-pointed needle got twisted around by mistake!

What a blast playing with this technique is! I think I've only scratched the surface of designing with wrapped stitches.

ELONGATING STITCHES

To play with wrapped stitches, we first need to create an extra-long, or elongated, stitch. If you wanted your stitch to be longer, you could work it more loosely, but this would make it hard to keep your gauge even. Another way to handle this is to take the yarn and wind it two or even three times around the needle. (Typically, when you work a stitch, you only wrap the yarn around the needle once, right?) When you drop these wraps on the next row, you've made a stitch that is twice or even three times the length of a "regular" stitch. Once you have an elongated stitch, there are many possibilities for playing with them.

Wrapping Stitch Twice

Insert the right-hand needle into the next stitch on the left-hand needle, wrap the yarn *twice* around the right-hand needle, at its widest circumference, and then complete the stitch as usual, either a knit or a purl stitch.

Wrapping Stitch Three Times

Insert the right-hand needle into the next stitch on the left-hand needle, wrap the yarn *three times* around the right-hand needle, at its widest circumference, and then complete the stitch as usual, either a knit or a purl stitch.

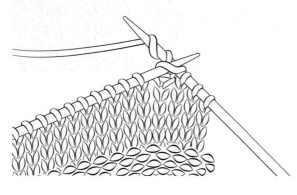

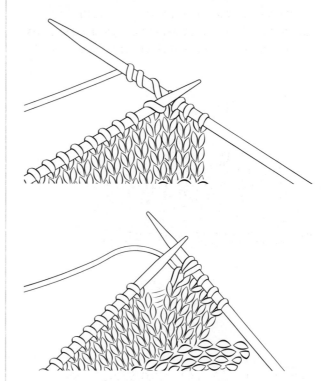

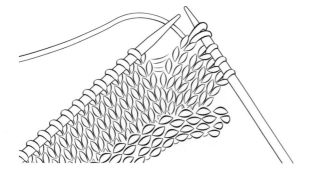

Dropping Extra Wraps

The most elementary way to work with wrapped stitches is to simply knit or purl them on the next row, which creates an open fabric. When you reach the extra wraps created in the previous row, slide the extra wrap(s) off the left-hand needle before working that stitch.

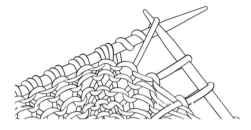

Knit (or Purl) Criss-Cross 4 (6)

This technique, as well as Opposite Purl Criss-Cross 4 (page 14), reorients multiple elongated stitches' positions on the needles so that they criss-cross over each other. Slip 1 stitch purlwise (dropping the extra wraps) 4 (6) times onto the right-hand needle. With the left-hand needle pass the first 2 (3) slipped stitches over the last 2 (3) slipped stitches and onto the left-hand needle. Move the remaining 2 (3) slipped stitches onto the left-hand needle. Knit (or purl) these 4 (6) stitches.

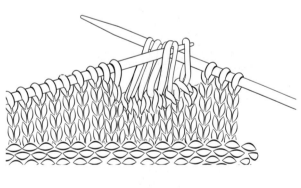

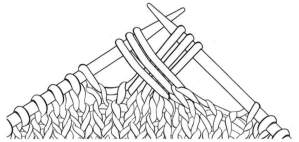

Opposite Purl Criss-Cross 4

Slip 1 stitch purlwise (dropping the extra wraps) 4 times onto the right-hand needle, move all 4 stitches back over to the left-hand needle. With the right-hand needle pass the first 2 slipped stitches over the last 2 slipped stitches, leaving them on the left-hand needle. Purl these 4 stitches.

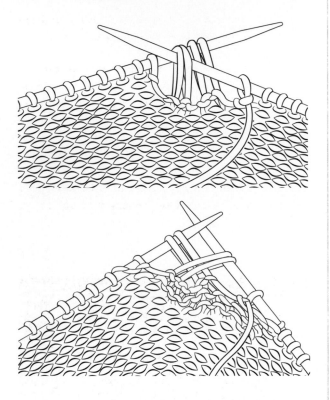

Across-6 (4, 3)

Use this technique to cross individual elongated stitches over each other. Drop the first stitch from the left-hand needle, leave it to the front of the work, and slip the next 4 (2, 1) stitches to the right-hand needle. Drop the next stitch, leaving it to the front of the work, and place the first stitch back onto the left-hand needle. Slip the 4 (2, 1) stitches from the right-hand needle back to the left-hand needle. Take the last dropped stitch and place it onto the left-hand needle. Knit these 6 (4, 3) stitches. Don't worry when dropping these stitches; since they have been elongated, they won't go anywhere. Just be careful when you pick them back up that the right leg of the stitch is to the front of the needle (i.e., don't twist it).

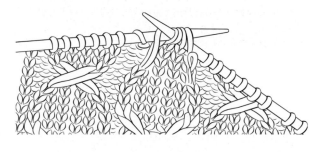

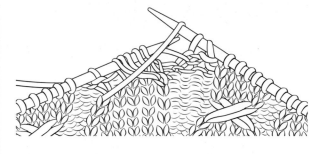

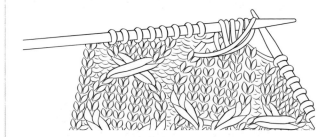

Open Split-6 (4)

This technique moves individual elongated stitches away from each other. Slip the next 2 (1) stitches onto the right-hand needle, drop the next stitch and leave to the front of the work, and slip 2 (1) stitches back to the left-hand needle. Pick up the dropped stitch, put it onto the left-hand needle, and knit these 3 (2) stitches. Drop the next stitch, leaving it to the front of the work, and slip the next 2 (1) stitches onto the right-hand needle. Pick up the dropped stitch and place it onto the left-hand needle, then slip 2 (1) stitches back to left-hand needle. Knit these 3 (2) stitches.

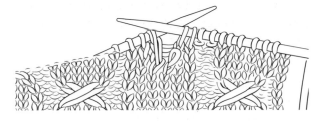

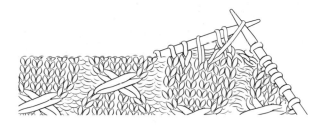

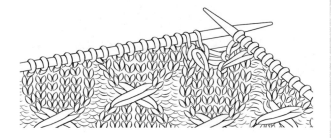

WRAPPING TIPS AND TRICKS

» Work wraps loosely. If you wrap tightly, they will not slide on the needle.

» Wrap yarn around the widest circumference of the needle, not around the needle tip.

» When you have wrapped stitches on the needle, *do not* pull down on your work as this will collapse the stitches and prevent them from sliding easily!

» Do not count wraps as extra stitches. All the wraps can make it difficult to check your stitch numbers on rows in which elongated stitches are worked. It's best to count your stitches on the following row, when all the stitches are restored to "normal."

A great starter project that introduces wrapped stitches, this funky cuff also highlights a favorite handmade button. You'll learn how to elongate stitches to create the pattern and an integrated buttonhole at the same time. How easy is that?

≫ I don't know about you, but I have stashes—there are yarn, bead, and even button stashes. This project helps me whittle down two out of those three stashes. I love wearing multiple versions together and this might be the fastest gift I've ever knit. I'd love to see the combinations that you come up with!

WAVE CUFF

Skill Level
Beginner

Materials
- 12 yd (11m) DK-weight yarn (3)
- US size 7 (4.5mm) needles, or size needed to obtain gauge
- Tapestry needle
- ¾" (2cm) oval porcelain button (Melissa Jean Design)

Yarn Used
Lion Brand *Cashmere;* 100% cashmere; 0.88 oz (25g), 82 yd (75m); 1 skein each in Cruise (106), Sprout (173), and Toffee (124)

Gauge
21 stitches and 32 rows = 4" (10cm) in stockinette stitch, blocked

Size
Small (Medium)
Shown in both sizes
The pattern is written for multiple lengths. Instructions are given for size small, with larger size in parentheses.

Finished Measurements
7 (8)" (18 [20.5]cm) long x 1¾" (4.5cm) wide

To Fit
5½ (6½)" (14 [16.5]cm) wrist circumference

CUFF

Using the long-tail method (page 138), cast on 32 (37) sts.

ROW 1: Knit all sts.

ROW 2: K8 (13), *k1 wrapping yarn twice, [k1 wrapping yarn 3 times] 3 times, k1 wrapping yarn twice, k3; repeat from * twice more.

ROW 3: Knit across, dropping extra wraps when you reach them.

ROWS 4 AND 5: Knit all sts.

ROW 6: K8 (13), k1 wrapping yarn twice, k3, k1 wrapping yarn twice, *[k1 wrapping yarn 3 times] 3 times, k1 wrapping yarn twice, k3, k1 wrapping yarn twice; rep from * once more, k1 wrapping yarn 3 times, k2.

ROW 7: Knit all sts, dropping extra wraps when you reach them.

ROWS 8 AND 9: Knit all sts.

ROW 10: Repeat Row 2.

ROW 11: Knit all sts, dropping extra wraps when you reach them.

ROW 12: Knit all sts.

Bind off loosely. Weave in ends and block (page 140) to measurements.

With right side facing, sew button onto the right edge of the garter stitch tab; see photo.

Take your wrapping skills up a notch by using multiple needle sizes to play with stitch length and density. This creates a ruched fabric. These mitts have a long cuff that can be worn pulled up or slouched down, and an integrated thumb gusset.

» As soon as these mitts came off the needles, my teenager began campaigning for a pair of her own (in black, of course). In my world her approval is pretty much the most accurate test of a successful design! Needless to say, we both will get our own version of this super-fast and functional knit.

PROLIX MITTS

Skill Level
Advanced Beginner

Materials
- 160 (180, 200) yd (146 [166, 183]m) worsted-weight yarn (4)
- US size 6 (4mm) double-pointed needles (or 1 long circular needle), or two sizes smaller than needed to obtain gauge
- US size 8 (5mm) double-pointed needles (or 1 long circular needle), or size needed to obtain gauge
- Stitch markers
- Scrap yarn (for stitch holder)
- Tapestry needle

Yarn Used
Lorna's Laces *Shepherd Worsted*; 100% merino wool; 4 oz (114g), 225 yd (206m); 1 skein in Chino

Gauge
18 stitches and 28 rounds = 4" (10cm) in stockinette stitch on larger needle, blocked

Size
Women's Small (Medium, Large)
Shown in Small
The pattern is written for multiple sizes. Instructions are given for size small, with larger sizes in parentheses.

Finished Measurements
7 (7½, 8¼)" (18 [19, 21]cm) hand circumference

CUFF

With smaller needles and the long-tail method (page 138), cast on 32 (34, 36) sts. Join for working in the round distributing sts on needles as preferred, being careful not to twist the sts. If desired, mark the beginning of the round with a removable stitch marker or safety pin.

ROUND 1: Knit all sts.

ROUND 2: Purl all sts.

Repeat these two rounds once more. Switch to larger needles.

ROUND 5: Knit all sts.

ROUND 6: Knit all sts, wrapping yarn twice for each st.

ROUND 7: Knit all sts, dropping extra wrap when you reach them. Switch to smaller needles.

ROUND 8: Knit all sts.

ROUND 9: Purl all sts.

Repeat the last two rounds once more. Switch to larger needles.

ROUND 12: Knit all sts.

ROUND 13: Knit all sts, wrapping yarn 3 times for each st.

ROUND 14: Knit all sts, dropping extra wraps when you reach them. Switch to smaller needles.

Repeat Rounds 1–14 twice more, then repeat Rounds 1–12 once more. Cuff measures approximately 8½" (21.5cm) from cast-on edge.

FINAL ROUND: Knit to the last st, k1f&b—33 (35, 37) sts.

SHAPE THUMB GUSSET

SET-UP ROUND: K16 (17, 18), place marker, m1R, k1, m1L, place marker, knit to end of round—35 (37, 39) sts.

Knit 2 rounds.

INCREASE ROUND: Knit to marker, sl marker, m1R, knit to next marker, m1L, sl marker, knit to end of round—2 sts increased.

Knit 2 rounds.

Repeat these last three rounds 3 (4, 4) times more—11 (13, 13) sts between markers.

NEXT ROUND: Knit to marker, remove marker, slip thumb gusset sts onto a length of scrap yarn, remove marker, cast on 1 st over gap left by gusset, and knit to end of round—33 (35, 37) sts.

Knit around until the piece measures 12 (12½, 13)" (30.5 [32, 33]cm) from cast-on edge.

Switch to smaller needles.

Purl 1 round.

Knit 1 round.

Bind off.

THUMB

With larger needles, return held thumb gusset sts to three needles, distributing sts as you prefer. With right side facing, rejoin yarn and pick up and k1 st tbl over gap and join for working in the round—12 (14, 14) sts.

Knit 4 (4, 5) rounds.

Switch to smaller needles.

Purl 1 round.

Knit 1 round.

Bind off.

Weave in ends, and use the tail at the base of the thumb to close up gaps at the thumb gusset.

Wet-block (page 140), and wear!

The band in this cloche is created with a twisted double wrap stitch that I invented to help this 1920s-inspired cloche fit properly. The Folly Cloche is worked from the top down in stockinette stitch and finished off with a short-row-shaped brim.

» A well-fitting cloche usually has a band that helps it sit snugly on the head, and I wanted to find an openwork stitch that would serve this purpose. The challenge was that open stitches normally make your gauge looser! I started to explore, twisting my needle all the way around, and realized that would tighten things up a bit.

FOLLY CLOCHE

Skill Level
Intermediate

Materials
- 145 (165, 185) yd (133 [151, 170]m) superwash worsted-weight yarn (4)
- US size 6 (4mm) double-pointed needles (or 1 long circular needle), or size needed to obtain gauge
- US size 6 (4mm) 16" (40cm) circular needle, or size needed to obtain gauge
- US size 7 (4.5mm) 16" (40cm) circular needle, or one size larger than needed to obtain gauge
- Stitch marker
- Tapestry needle

Yarn Used
Jill Draper Makes Stuff *Hudson;* 100% merino wool; 4 oz (113g), 240 yd (219m); 1 skein in Cinnabar

Gauge
21 stitches and 28 rounds = 4" (10cm) in stockinette stitch on smaller needle, blocked

Size
Small (Medium, Large)
Shown in Medium
The pattern is written for multiple sizes. Instructions are given for size small, with larger sizes in parentheses.

Finished Measurements
18¼ (20, 21¼)" (46 [51, 54]cm) around, unstretched

Notes
- This cloche should fit snugly, so choose a size that is approximately 1½" (3.8cm) smaller than your desired head circumference.

- You will have better success with the fit of this hat if you use a superwash yarn, as it is more elastic and will stretch better when you work the twisted stitch in the brim.

CROWN

Using the smaller needle, cast on 8 sts with a circular cast-on (page 139).

Slide the sts to the other end of the needle and knit 1 row distributing sts evenly over your needles as preferred. Join for working in the round, being careful not to twist the sts. If desired, mark the beginning of the round with a removable stitch marker or safety pin.

ROUND 1: *K1f&b; rep from * to end of round—16 sts.

ROUND 2 AND ALL EVEN ROUNDS: Knit all sts.

ROUND 3: *K2, m1R; rep from * to end of round—24 sts.

ROUND 5: *K3, m1R; rep from * to end of round—32 sts.

ROUND 7: *K4, m1R; rep from * to end of round—40 sts.

ROUND 9: *K5, m1R; rep from * to end of round—48 sts.

ROUND 11: *K6, m1R; rep from * to end of round—56 sts.

ROUND 13: *K7, m1R; rep from * to end of round—64 sts.

ROUND 15: *K8, m1R; rep from * to end of round—72 sts.

ROUND 17: *K9, m1R; rep from * to end of round—80 sts.

ROUND 19: *K10, m1R; rep from * to end of round—88 sts.

ROUND 21: *K11, m1R; rep from * to end of round—96 sts.

NOTE: If you are working on double-pointed needles and your stitches become crowded, change to a circular needle of the same size, placing marker for the start of the round. If you are working Magic Loop (page 137), you can switch to a circular needle of the same size, placing marker for the start of the round, if preferred.

Medium and Large Only
ROUND 22: Knit all sts.

ROUND 23: *K12, m1R; rep from * to end of round—104 sts.

Large Only
ROUND 24: Knit all sts.

ROUND 25: *K13, m1R; rep from * to end of round—112 sts.

All Sizes
Knit 12 (15, 17) more rounds.

Short-Row Shaping
ROW 1 (RS): Knit to 12 sts before marker, W&T.

ROW 2 (WS): Purl to 12 sts before marker, W&T.

ROW 3: Knit to 18 sts before marker, W&T.

ROW 4: Purl to 18 sts before marker, W&T.

ROW 5: Knit to 24 sts before marker, W&T.

ROW 6: Purl to 24 sts before marker, W&T.

ROW 7: Knit to 30 sts before marker, W&T.

ROW 8: Purl to 30 sts before marker, W&T.

ROW 9: Knit to the end of the round, working wraps together with wrapped sts as you encounter them.

NEXT ROUND: Knit to end of round, working wraps together with wrapped sts as you encounter them.

Switch to the larger circular needle.

BAND

ROUND 1: Knit all sts wrapping yarn twice for each st.

ROUND 2: *Slip 4 sts purlwise onto a double-pointed needle dropping extra wraps, twist needle 360° clockwise, knit 4 sts from double-pointed needle; rep from * to end of round.

ROUND 3: Knit all sts.

ROUND 4: Repeat Round 1.

ROUND 5: *Slip 2 sts purlwise, dropping wraps onto the right-hand needle, slip 4 sts onto a double-pointed needle dropping extra wraps, twist needle 360° clockwise, knit 4 sts from the double-pointed needle; rep from * around to last 2 sts, slip the last 2 sts purlwise dropping wraps onto the double-pointed needle, slip marker, and slip the next two sts purlwise onto the double-pointed needle, twist needle 360° clockwise, knit 4 sts from the double-pointed needle, slipping marker when you reach it.

ROUND 6: Knit to end of round.

ROUNDS 7 AND 8: Repeat Rounds 1 and 2.

ROUND 9: Knit all sts.

INCREASE ROUND: K26 (27, 25), k1f&b, [k2, k1f&b] 14 (16, 20) times, knit to end of round—111 (121, 133) sts.

Short-Row Shaping for Brim

ROW 1 (RS): Knit to 18 sts before marker, W&T.

ROW 2 (WS): Purl to 18 sts before marker, W&T.

ROW 3: Knit to 24 sts before marker, W&T.

ROW 4: Purl to 24 sts before marker, W&T.

ROW 5: Knit to 30 sts before marker, W&T.

ROW 6: Purl to 30 sts before marker, W&T.

ROW 7: Knit to end of round, working wraps together with wrapped sts as you encounter them.

NEXT ROUND: Knit to end of round, working wraps together with wrapped sts as you encounter them.

I-CORD BIND-OFF

Using the knit cast-on method (page 139), cast on 2 sts onto the left-hand needle.

*K1, slip 1 knitwise, k1 from the brim of the hat, psso, slip 2 sts from the right-hand needle back to the left-hand needle; rep from * until 2 sts remain, k2tog.

Cut yarn leaving an 8" (20.5cm) tail, pull through last stitch worked.

With this tail join the beginning and end of the I-cord edging together.

Weave in all ends and block (page 140). If your brim does not lie flat, you can steam it flat with a damp towel and a warm iron.

A loose-fitting hat, this project shows you what else those elongated stitches can do. Worked from the bottom up, it features a faux cable rib stitch that is created by manipulating elongated stitches. The elasticity of the stitch allows the hat to fit a variety of head sizes, making this a versatile, giftable knit!

» I don't regularly design for men, and with Laxo Hat I wanted to remedy that. This hat is for all of you who want to knit something more sedate and yet wearable. Keep in mind that this hat does best with a bit of drape, so if you have a precious skein of cashmere sock yarn lying around, now is the time to break it out.

LAXO HAT

Skill Level
Advanced Beginner

Materials
- 235 yd (214m) fingering-weight yarn [1]
- US size 2 (2.75mm) 16" (40cm) circular needle, or one size smaller than needed to obtain gauge
- US size 3 (3.25mm) 16" (40cm) circular needle, or size needed to obtain gauge
- US size 3 (3.25mm) double-pointed needles (or 1 long circular needle), or size needed to obtain gauge
- Stitch marker
- Tapestry needle

Yarn Used
Jill Draper Makes Stuff *Splendor Sock Yarn;* 80% merino, 10% cashmere, 10% nylon; 3½ oz (100g), 435 yd (398m); 1 skein in Antique Mahogany

Gauge
24 stitches and 32 rounds = 4" (10cm) in stockinette stitch on larger needle, blocked
27 stitches and 32 rounds = 4" (10cm) in pattern stitch on larger needle, blocked

Size
To fit an average adult head; stretches up to 23" (58.5cm) in circumference

Finished Measurements
19" (48.5cm) around, unstretched

Note
- Slip all sts purlwise.

HAT

With the smaller circular needle and the long-tail method (page 138), cast on 144 sts, place marker and join for working in the round, being careful not to twist the sts.

RIBBING ROUND: *P2, k2: rep from * to end of round.

Work Ribbing as established for 8 more rounds.

Hat Body

Switch to the larger circular needle and begin to work the Hat Body as follows:

ROUND 1: *P2, k1 wrapping yarn twice, k4, k1 wrapping yarn twice, p2, k6; rep from * to end of round.

ROUNDS 2 AND 3: *P2, sl1, k4, sl1, p2, k6; rep from * to end of round.

(Slip all sts purlwise. On the first of the last 2 rounds, drop extra wraps when you reach them.)

ROUND 4: *P2, across-6, p2, k6; rep from * to end of round.

ROUND 5: *P2, k6, p2, k2, [k1 wrapping yarn twice] twice, k2; rep from * to end of round.

ROUNDS 6 AND 7: *P2, k6, p2, k2, sl2, k2; rep from * to end of round.

(On the first of the last 2 rounds, drop extra wraps when you reach them.)

ROUND 8: *P2, k6, p2, open split-6; rep from * to end of round.

ROUND 9: *P2, k2, [k1 wrapping yarn twice] twice, k2, p2, k6; rep from * to end of round.

ROUNDS 10 AND 11: *P2, k2, sl2, k2, p2, k6; rep from * to end of round.

(On the first of the last 2 rounds, drop extra wraps when you reach them.)

ROUND 12: *P2, open split-6, p2, k6; rep from * to end of round.

ROUND 13: *P2, k6, p2, k1 wrapping yarn twice, k4, k1 wrapping yarn twice; rep from * to end of round.

ROUNDS 14 AND 15: *P2, k6, p2, sl1, k4, sl1; rep from * to end of round.

(On the first of the last 2 rounds, drop extra wraps when you reach them.)

ROUND 16: *P2, k6, p2, across-6; rep from * to end of round.

Work Rounds 1–16 twice more, then work Rounds 1–8 once more.

Hat should measure approximately 7" (18cm) from cast-on edge.

Crown Decreases

NOTE: When the sts start to stretch on the needle, switch to double-pointed needles or the Magic Loop technique.

ROUND 1: *P2, k2tog, [k1 wrapping yarn twice] twice, k2tog, p2, k6; rep from * around—126 sts remain.

ROUNDS 2 AND 3: *P2, k1, sl2, k1, p2, k6; rep from * to end of round.

(On the first of the last 2 rounds, drop extra wraps when you reach them.)

ROUND 4: *P2, open split-4, p2, k6; rep from * to end of round.

ROUND 5: *P2, k4, p2, k1 wrapping yarn twice, k2tog twice, k1 wrapping yarn twice; rep from * to end of round—108 sts remain.

ROUNDS 6 AND 7: *P2, k4, p2, sl1, k2, sl1; rep from * to end of round.

(On the first of the last 2 rounds, drop extra wraps when you reach them.)

ROUND 8: *P2, k6, p2, across-4; rep from * to end of round.

ROUND 9: *P2, k1 wrapping yarn twice, k2tog, k1 wrapping yarn twice, p2, k1, k2tog, k1; rep from * to end of round—90 sts remain.

ROUND 10: *P2, sl1, k1, sl1, p2, k3; rep from * to end of round. (Drop extra wraps when you reach them.)

ROUND 11: *P2tog, sl1, k1, sl1, p2tog, k3; rep from * to end of round—72 sts remain.

ROUND 12: *P1, across-3, p1, k3; rep from * to end of round.

ROUND 13: *P1, k2tog, k1; rep from * to end of round—54 sts remain.

ROUND 14: *P1, k2tog; rep from * to end of round—36 sts remain.

ROUND 15: *K2tog; rep from * to end of round—18 sts remain.

ROUND 16: *K2tog; rep from * to end of round—9 sts remain.

Cut yarn leaving an 8" (20.5cm) tail, thread through remaining live sts to close up the top of the hat.

Weave in all ends and block (page 140).

These toppers are the perfect project to learn the elongated stitch criss-cross technique. And they're so quick, you'll want to make a pair for all your fashionable friends! Meant to be worn over boots, toppers help prevent the cold air from creeping in. The bulky yarn and fat ribbing make them quite stretchy, and perfect for gift giving.

» I never saw the wisdom in boot toppers until one winter when I received a pair from my friend Kate. Finally, here was a way to wear leggings and dresses throughout harsh Ithaca winters and not freeze at the same time. Now I have quite a collection. I love not wearing pants all winter long!

BOOTSY BOOT TOPPERS

Skill Level
Advanced Beginner

Materials
- 120 (150) yd (110 [137]m) bulky-weight yarn (5)
- US size 11 (8mm) double-pointed needles (or 1 long circular needle), or size needed to obtain gauge
- Stitch marker
- Tapestry needle

Yarn Used
Brown Sheep *Lamb's Pride Bulky*; 85% wool, 15% mohair; 4 oz (113g), 125 yd (114m); 1 (2) skein(s) in Winter Blue (M-51)

Gauge
12 stitches and 18 rows = 4" (10cm) in stockinette stitch, blocked
14 stitches and 16 rounds = 4" (10cm) in ribbing, blocked

Size
Stretches to fit around leg up to 15 (18)" (38 [45.5]cm) in circumference
The pattern is written for multiple sizes. Instructions are given for size small, with larger size in parentheses.

Finished Measurements
12 (15)" (30.5 [38]cm) top-to-bottom circumference x 8" (20.5cm) high

CUFF

Using the long-tail method (page 138), cast on 40 (50) sts and join for working in the round distributing sts on needles as preferred, being careful not to twist the sts. Mark the beginning of the round with a removable stitch marker or safety pin.

ROUND 1: Purl to end of round.

ROUND 2: *K1, wrapping yarn 3 times; rep from * to end of round.

ROUND 3: *Knit Criss-Cross 6, Knit Criss-Cross 4; rep from * to end of round.

ROUND 4: Purl to end of round.

ROUND 5: Knit to end of round.

ROUND 6: Purl to end of round.

LEG

RIBBING ROUND: *K3, p2; rep from * to end of round.

Work Ribbing as established until boot topper measures 8" (20.5cm) from cast-on or desired length.

Bind off loosely in pattern.

Weave in ends and block (page 140).

This triangular shawl is constructed in pieces: two mirrored triangles are knit individually and then joined by a symmetrical center panel. The open fabric is created by elongated stitches with decorative criss-crosses at the edges; practice the beginner's version of this stitch by making the Bootsy Boot Toppers (page 31). A gradient yarn with long color repeats keeps the knitting interesting and makes the shawl look more complex than it is!

» Multiple times a year I run Mystery Knit-Alongs in my Ravelry group. My goal with these Mystery Knit-Alongs is to surprise the participants with unexpected constructions so they don't know right away what they are making. I used this three-part construction for Kinetik, a double-sided lace shawl with beads. I've known ever since that I wanted to translate it into a simpler, more relaxed shawl.

LAS CRUCES SHAWL

Skill Level
Intermediate

Materials
• 625 yd (572m) light fingering-weight yarn 🔟
• 2 US size 6 (4mm) 24" (60cm) (or longer) circular needles, or size needed to obtain gauge
• Tapestry needle

Yarn Used
Noro *Taiyo Sock;* 50% cotton, 17% wool, 17% nylon, 16% silk; 3½ oz (100g), 462 yd (422m); 2 skeins in color 25

Gauge
22 stitches and 32 rows = 4" (10cm) in stockinette stitch, blocked
19 stitches and 23 rows = 4" (10cm) in pattern stitch, blocked

Finished Measurements
Approximately 70" (178cm) wide across top edge x 22" (56cm) long at center

Note
• The colors in the sample project flow gradually from one to another. This is not always the case with Noro yarns, since sometimes there is a color change on the skein due to the manufacturing process. If you start with a full two skeins you will have more than enough yarn to "move" forward on the skein to find the next color repeat if you want to avoid abrupt changes.

RIGHT TRIANGLE

Setup

Using the knitted-on method (page 139), cast on 6 sts.

ROW 1 (RS): Knit to the last 2 sts, k1f&b, k1—7 sts.

ROW 2 (WS): Knit to end of row.

ROW 3: Knit to the last st, m1L, k1—8 sts.

ROW 4: Knit to end of row.

ROW 5: Knit to the last st, wrapping yarn twice for each st, m1L wrapping yarn twice, k1 wrapping yarn twice—9 sts.

ROW 6: Dropping extra wraps, purl to the last 4 sts, Purl Criss-Cross 4.

Body

ROW 1: Purl to the last st, m1L, k1—1 st increased.

ROW 2: Purl to end of row.

ROW 3: Knit to the last st, m1L, k1—1 st increased.

ROW 4: Knit to end of row.

ROW 5: Knit to the last st, wrapping yarn twice for each st, m1L wrapping yarn twice, k1 wrapping yarn twice—1 st increased.

ROW 6: Dropping extra wraps, p2, Purl Criss-Cross 4, purl to the last 4 sts, Purl Criss-Cross 4.

Repeat Rows 1–6 twenty-five times more—87 sts.

Work Rows 1–4 once more—89 sts.

Cut yarn, leaving a 6" (15cm) tail, leave sts on needle and set aside.

LEFT TRIANGLE

Setup

Using the knitted-on method (page 139), cast on 6 sts.

ROW 1 (WS): Purl to the last 2 sts, p1f&b, p1—7 sts.

ROW 2 (RS): Purl to end of row.

ROW 3: Purl to the last st, m1L purlwise, p1—8 sts.

ROW 4: Purl to end of row.

ROW 5: Purl to the last st, wrapping yarn twice for each st, m1L purlwise wrapping yarn twice, p1 wrapping yarn twice—9 sts.

ROW 6: Dropping extra wraps, knit to the last 4 sts, Knit Criss-Cross 4.

Body

ROW 1: Knit to the last st, m1L purlwise, p1—1 st increased.

ROW 2: Knit to end of row.

ROW 3: Purl to the last st, m1L purlwise, p1—1 st increased.

ROW 4: Purl to end of row.

ROW 5: Purl to the last st, wrapping yarn twice for each st, m1L purlwise wrapping yarn twice, p1 wrapping yarn twice—1 st increased.

ROW 6: Dropping extra wraps, k2, Knit Criss-Cross 4, knit to the last 4 sts, Knit Criss-Cross 4.

Repeat Rows 1–6 twenty-five times more—87 sts.

Work Rows 1–4 once more—89 sts.

Without cutting yarn, continue on to Center Joining Panel.

JOINING LEFT AND RIGHT TRIANGLES WITH CENTER PANEL

With needle holding sts of Left Triangle in left hand (right side facing) and using the knitted-on method (page 139), cast on 50 sts.

Setup

ROW 1 (RS): K49, sl1 knitwise with yarn in back, k1 (from live sts on held Left Triangle), psso. Turn—138 sts.

ROW 2 (WS): Sl1 purlwise with yarn in front, k48, sl1 purlwise with yarn in front, p1 from held sts on Right Triangle, psso. Turn—226 sts.

ROW 3: Sl1 purlwise with yarn in back, k48 wrapping yarn twice for each st, sl1 knitwise with yarn in back, k1 (from Left Triangle), psso. Turn—225 sts.

ROW 4: Sl1 purlwise with yarn in front, Purl Criss-Cross 4 twelve times, sl1 purlwise with yarn in front, p1 (from Right Triangle), psso. Turn—224 sts.

Body

ROW 1: Sl1 purlwise with yarn in back, p48, sl1 knitwise with yarn in back, k1 (from Left Triangle), psso. Turn—1 st decreased.

ROW 2: Sl1 purlwise with yarn in front, p48, sl1 purlwise with yarn in front, p1 (from Right Triangle), psso. Turn—1 st decreased.

ROW 3: Sl1 purlwise with yarn in back, k48, sl1 knitwise with yarn in back, k1 (from Left Triangle), psso. Turn—1 st decreased.

ROW 4: Sl1 purlwise with yarn in front, k48, sl1 purlwise with yarn in front, p1 (from Right Triangle), psso. Turn—1 st decreased.

ROW 5: Sl1 purlwise with yarn in back, k48 wrapping yarn twice, sl1 knitwise with yarn in back, k1 (from Left Triangle), psso. Turn—1 st decreased.

ROW 6: Sl1 purlwise with yarn in front, p48 dropping extra wraps, sl1 purlwise with yarn in front, p1 (from Right Triangle), psso. Turn—1 st decreased.

Repeat Rows 1–6 twenty-seven times more. Repeat Rows 1–4 once more—52 sts.

ROW 169: Sl1 purlwise with yarn in back, k48, sl1 knitwise with yarn in back, k1 (from Left Triangle), psso. Turn—51 sts.

ROW 170: Sl1 purlwise with yarn in front, k48, sl1 purlwise with yarn in front, p1 (from Right Triangle), psso. Turn—50 sts.

Bind off remaining 50 sts of Center Panel loosely. Weave in ends, and wet-block (page 140) to measurements.

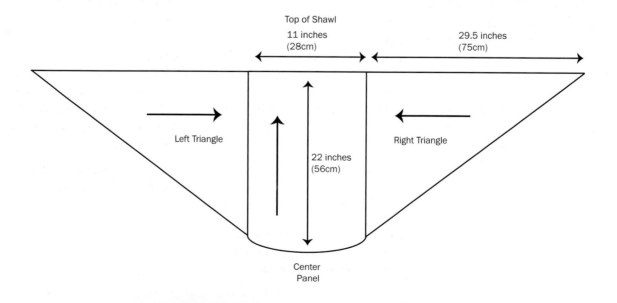

Top of Shawl

11 inches
(28cm)

29.5 inches
(75cm)

Left Triangle

Right Triangle

22 inches
(56cm)

Center
Panel

Twisted stitches combined with elongated criss-crosses create a distinctive, stretchy sock fabric. The criss-cross is echoed at each edge of the heel flap, making this sock design a bit unexpected and enjoyable to knit!

≫ Many knitters (myself included) are drawn to wildly fun, hand-dyed skeins, but aren't quite sure what to do with them. Some hand-dyes create unexpected pools of color when they are knit. Luckily, by crossing elongated stitches in the Traversus Socks we can resolve this dilemma by distracting the eye from any color pooling that might occur. I love creating stitch patterns that take advantage of the unique characteristics of variegated hand-dyed yarn.

TRAVERSUS SOCKS

Skill Level
Advanced Intermediate

Materials
- 325 (350, 400) yd (300 [320, 365]m) fingering-weight yarn (1)
- US size 1 (2.25mm) double-pointed needles (or 1 long circular needle), or 1 size smaller than needed to obtain gauge
- US size 1.5 (2.5mm) double-pointed needles (or 1 long circular needle), or size needed to obtain gauge
- Stitch marker
- Tapestry needle

Yarn Used
Madelinetosh *Tosh Sock;* 100% superwash merino wool; 4 oz (113g), 395 yd (361m); 1 (1, 2) skeins in Grenadine

Gauge
30 stitches and 44 rounds = 4" (10cm) in stockinette stitch on larger needle, blocked
40 stitches and 40 rounds = 4" (10cm) in leg pattern stitch on larger needle, unstretched, blocked

Size
Small (Medium, Large)
Shown in Small
The pattern is written for multiple sizes. Instructions are given for size small, with larger sizes in parentheses.

Finished Measurements
7 (7½, 8)" (18 [19, 20.5]cm) foot circumference, 7" (18cm) long from Instep to Cuff
Leg length and foot length are adjustable to fit

Notes
- The stitch pattern used in this sock is very stretchy, so the unstretched sock should be approximately 1½" (4cm) smaller than the desired foot circumference.

- Leg circumference for sizes Small and Medium is the same.

CUFF

With smaller needles and using the long-tail method (page 138), cast on 66 (66, 77) sts, and join for working in the round distributing sts on needles as preferred, being careful not to twist the sts. Mark the beginning of the round with a removable stitch marker or safety pin.

Ribbing

ROUNDS 1-10: *K2tbl, p3, k3tbl, p2, k1tbl; rep from * to end of round.

ROUND 11: *K2tbl, p1, p2tog, k3tbl, p2, k1tbl; rep from * to end of round—60 (60, 70) sts.

LEG

Switch to larger needles.

ROUND 1: *K2tbl, p2, k2tbl, [k1 wrapping yarn twice] 4 times; rep from * to end of round.

ROUND 2: *K2tbl, p2, k2tbl, Knit Criss-Cross 4; rep from * to end of round.

ROUND 3: *K1tbl, [k1 wrapping yarn twice] 4 times, k2tbl, p2, k1tbl; rep from * to end of round.

ROUND 4: *K1tbl, Knit Criss-Cross 4, k2tbl, p2, k1tbl; rep from * to end of round.

Work Rounds 1–4 until leg measures 7" (18cm) from cast-on edge, ending with Round 1.

FINAL ROUND: Work in pattern as established to 1 st before end of round—this is the starting position for the heel flap. The heel flap is worked back and forth over the next 28 (28, 38) sts—rearrange sts as you prefer. Remaining 32 (32, 32) sts will be worked later for instep.

HEEL FLAP

Work heel stitches back and forth in rows as follows:

Small Only

ROW 1 (RS): *K2tbl, [k1 wrapping yarn twice] 4 times, k2tbl, p2; rep from * once more, k2tbl, [k1 wrapping yarn twice] 4 times, k2tbl, turn—28 sts.

ROW 2 (WS): Sl1 purlwise with yarn in front, p1tbl, Opposite Purl Criss-Cross 4, *p2tbl, k2, p2tbl, Opposite Purl Criss-Cross 4; rep from * once more, p2tbl.

Medium Only

ROW 1 (RS): *K2tbl, [k1 wrapping yarn twice] 4 times, k2tbl, m1R, p2, m1L; rep from * once more, k2tbl, [k1 wrapping yarn twice] 4 times, k2tbl, turn—32 sts.

ROW 2 (WS): Sl1 purlwise with yarn in front, p1tbl, Opposite Purl Criss-Cross 4, *p3tbl, k2, p3tbl, Opposite Purl Criss-Cross 4; rep from * once more, p2tbl.

Large Only

ROW 1 (RS): *K2tbl, [k1 wrapping yarn twice] 4 times, k2tbl, p2; rep from * twice more, k2tbl, [k1 wrapping yarn twice] 4 times, k2tbl, turn—38 sts.

ROW 2 (WS): Sl1 purlwise with yarn in front, p1tbl, Opposite Purl Criss-Cross 4, *p2tbl, k2, p2tbl, Opposite Purl Criss-Cross 4; rep from * twice more, p2tbl.

All Sizes

ROW 3 (RS): Sl1 knitwise with yarn in back, k1, k1tbl, p2, k1tbl, *sl1 knitwise, k1; rep from * to last 6 sts, k1tbl, p2, k1tbl, k2.

ROW 4 (WS): Sl1 purlwise with yarn in front, p1, p1tbl, k2, p1tbl, purl to last 6 sts, p1tbl, k2, p1tbl, p2.

ROW 5: Sl1 knitwise with yarn in back, k1, [k1 wrapping yarn twice] 4 times, *sl1 knitwise, k1; rep from * to last 6 sts, [k1 wrapping yarn twice] 4 times, k2.

ROW 6: Sl1 purlwise with yarn in front, p1, Opposite Purl Criss-Cross 4, purl to last 6 sts, Opposite Purl Criss-Cross 4, p2.

Repeat Rows 3–6 six (six, seven) times more, then work Rows 3 and 4 zero (one, zero) time more—30 (32, 34) rows total, 15 (16, 17) slipped edge sts at each selvedge.

TURN HEEL

Work short rows to shape heel as follows:

ROW 1 (RS): Sl1 purlwise with yarn in back, k15 (17, 20), ssk, k1, turn.

ROW 2 (WS): Sl1 purlwise with yarn in front, p5, p2tog, p1, turn.

ROW 3: Sl1 purlwise with yarn in back, knit to 1 st before the gap produced by the previous row, ssk (using 1 st from each side of the gap), k1, turn.

ROW 4: Sl1 purlwise with yarn in front, purl to 1 st before the gap produced by the previous row, p2tog (using 1 st from each side of the gap), p1, turn.

Repeat Rows 3 and 4 three (four, six) more times—18 (20, 22) sts remain.

Small and Medium Only

NEXT ROW (RS): Sl1 purlwise with yarn in back, knit to 1 st before the gap produced by the previous row, ssk (using 1 st from each side of the gap), turn.

FINAL ROW (WS): Sl1 purlwise with yarn in front, purl to 1 st before the gap produced by the previous row, p2tog (using 1 st from each side of the gap)—16 (18) heel sts remain.

GUSSET

The Gusset returns to working in the round as follows:

SETUP ROUND: K16 (18, 22) heel sts; pick up and knit 16 (17, 18) sts along the first edge of the heel flap; [p2, k3tbl] six times, p2 (instep sts); pick up and knit 16 (17, 18) sts along the second edge of the heel flap, k8 (9, 11) to center of Heel—80 (84, 90) sts.

(This is the new beginning of the round. Rearrange sts and/or place a marker as desired.)

GUSSET ROUND 1: Knit to 3 sts before the Instep, k2tog, k1, [p2, k3tbl] 6 times, p2; k1, ssk, knit to end of round—2 sts decreased.

GUSSET ROUND 2: Knit to the Instep, [p2, k3tbl] six times, p2, knit to end of round.

Repeat Gusset Rounds 1 and 2 nine (nine, ten) more times—60 (64, 68) sts remain.

FOOT

Work even in pattern as established until sock measures 2" (5cm) less than desired total foot length from back of Heel.

TOE

Set Up for Toe

Sts need to be rearranged so that there are 30 (32, 34) sts on the Sole and 30 (32, 34) sts on the Instep.

K15 (16, 17) (this is the start of the Instep—place a marker or divide sts at this point), k30 (32, 34) (this is the end of the Instep—place a marker or divide sts at this point), k15 (16, 17) to end of round.

All Sizes

ROUND 1: Knit to 3 sts before Instep, k2tog, k1; k1, ssk, knit to 3 sts before end of Instep, k2tog, k1; k1, ssk, knit to end of round—4 sts decreased.

ROUND 2: Knit to end of round.

Work Rounds 1 and 2 five (six, seven) more times—36 sts remain.

Work Round 1 five times—16 sts remain.

Knit to start of the Instep sts.

FINISHING

Cut yarn, leaving a 12" (30.5cm) tail. Thread tail on a tapestry needle and using Kitchener stitch (page 138), graft the remaining sts together. Weave in loose ends. Block lightly (page 140).

Worked in the round, the Crux Cowl alternates the elongated Criss-Cross stitch with twisted and dropped stitches to create a fabric of textural columns. The pattern includes two sizes, since sometimes a taller cowl is just what the doctor ordered!

》 Ever since Kate Gilbert released her infamous Clapotis scarf, I have been drawn to designs with dropped stitches. While designing the stitch for this cowl I suddenly realized it would be a blast to incorporate them. My absolute favorite part is watching the fabric open up as the stitches are dropped. Addictive, to be sure!

CRUX COWL

Skill Level
Intermediate

Materials
- 145 (250) yd (133 [230]m) DK-weight yarn (3)
- US size 6 (4mm) 24" (60cm) circular needle, or size needed to obtain gauge
- Stitch marker
- Tapestry needle

Yarn Used
The Fibre Company *Acadia;* 60% merino wool, 20% silk, 20% alpaca; 1¾ oz (50g), 145 yd (133m); 1 (2) skeins in Maple

Size
Small (Large)
Shown in Large
The pattern is written for multiple sizes. Instructions are given for size small, with larger size in parentheses.

Finished Measurements
18 (22)" (45.5 [56]cm) around x 10½ (15)" (26.5 [38]cm) high

Gauge
20 stitches and 28 rounds = 4" (10cm) in stockinette stitch, blocked
20 stitches and 17 rounds = 4" (10cm) in crux stitch, blocked

COWL

Using the crochet cast-on (page 138), cast on 90 (110) sts, place marker and join for working in the round, being careful not to twist the sts.

RIBBING ROUND: *P1, k1tbl, p2, k1tbl; rep from * to end of round.

Work ribbing round 4 times more.

SETUP ROUND: *Yo, k2togtbl, p2, k1tbl; rep from * to end of round.

Begin Crux Stitch

ROUND 1: *K1, k1tbl, p2, k1tbl, k1, k4 wrapping yarn twice; rep from * to end of round.

ROUND 2: *K1, k1tbl, p2, k1tbl, k1, Knit Criss-Cross 4; rep from * to end of round.

ROUND 3: *K1, k4 wrapping yarn twice, k1, k1tbl, p2, k1tbl; rep from * to end of round.

ROUND 4: *K1, knit Criss-Cross 4, k1, k1tbl, p2, k1tbl; rep from * to end of round.

Repeat Rounds 1–4 eight (thirteen) times more. Repeat Rounds 1 and 2 once more.

NEXT ROUND (DROP STITCHES): *Drop the next st off the left-hand needle, purl into front and then knit into back of next st, p2, k1tbl; rep from * to end of round.

NOTE: After working this round you can then "massage" all the dropped sts to release the floats.

RIBBING ROUND: *P1, k1tbl, p2, k1tbl; rep from * to end of round.

Work the Ribbing Round 4 times more.

Bind off in pattern loosely, working the knit sts through the front loop so that they don't tighten up.

Weave in ends and block (page 140).

2

GET *your* LACE ON

I adore knitting that engages my mind as well as my hands. Most lacework demands that my attention stay focused on the movement and rhythm of knitting. I love watching the process as the fabric grows off my needles, and then again when it's time to block. For the most part, lace looks like a crumpled blob until it's had a good soak and a stretch on a blocking board, allowing your lace to blossom into the gorgeous creature that it is. This transformation never ceases to amaze me. I'll spend a month knitting a shawl in delicate laceweight yarn (see the Loco Shawl, page 77) just for that magical moment.

My goal with this chapter is to start with a simple design to get you comfortable with the concept of working lace stitches. We'll look at chart-reading skills (no worries, many of the charts have written instructions, too), single- and then double-sided lace, and lace stitches that change in count from row to row so that the stitches shape the fabric. You'll find that you can knit lace, and then we'll build on those skills so you can wow yourself!

WHAT IS LACE?

Lace is a fabric built with strategically placed increases and decreases that make an airy, textured fabric. Typically, lace is knit on a needle a few sizes larger than recommended for the yarn's weight to create lace's characteristic drape. Lace stitches can form an overall texture, or draw an image, such as floral motifs or (my favorite) graphic geometric shapes.

Types of Lace

Some lace pieces only have lace worked on the right-side row, with wrong-side rows (or "rest rows") that are either knit or purled. This is known as single-sided lace. Double-sided lace features lace stitches on both the right-side and wrong-side rows. Knitting lace on two sides is more challenging, especially when you are working flat, but the final result is stunning because the yarn overs are able to stack upon one another. We'll explore both types in this chapter: Gateway Cuff (page 51) is an excellent example of single-sided lace, whereas the edgings on the Fornido Shawlette (page 57) and the Loco Shawl (page 77) play with the double-sided technique.

LACE TIPS AND TRICKS

» Mark the front of the work with a removable stitch marker.

» If a stitch pattern is challenging, start small with just one repeat. Practice until it "clicks"!

» If you are still struggling with a stitch pattern or cast-on, try it with bulkier yarn and bigger needles first. Once you have the concept down, it's time to try again with the project yarn.

» Use lifelines (page 49) and remember to mark on your pattern where you placed them.

» Mark up the lace chart to make it easier to read (page 48).

» Use stitch markers! Most of my lace patterns tell you where and when to place markers for each repeat. Breaking the pattern into smaller sections makes it easier to count stitches and keep track of where you are.

YARN OVERS

The yarn over is the most basic lace increase, but sometimes yarn overs throw knitters for a loop (pardon the pun) when they are used in unexpected ways. I'll walk you through four different scenarios.

A yarn over should *always* have its right leg to the front of the needle and its left leg to the back. This is true whether you knit continental or English (i.e., wrap with your left hand or throw with your right hand). Otherwise, the yarn over will twist and won't create a "hole" in the lacework. The goal is to wrap the yarn around the right-hand needle at its widest circumference.

Knit—Yarn Over—Knit
Knit 1 stitch, then bring the yarn to the front between the needles. Bring the yarn up and over the right-hand needle, leaving it to the back of the right-hand needle so you can knit the next stitch.

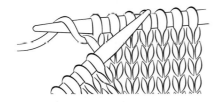

Knit—Yarn Over—Purl
Knit 1 stitch, then bring the yarn to the front between the needles. Bring the yarn up and over the right-hand needle, then bring it back to the front of the right-hand needle so you can purl the next stitch.

Purl—Yarn Over—Purl
Purl 1 stitch, then bring the yarn up and over the right-hand needle and back to the front of the right-hand needle so you can purl the next stitch.

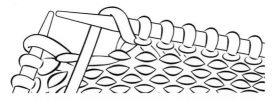

Purl—Yarn Over—Knit
Purl 1 stitch, then bring the yarn up and over the right-hand needle and leave it to the back of the right-hand needle so you can knit the next stitch.

Yarn Over Twice (or Double Yarn Over)
Wrap the yarn *twice* around the right-hand needle, at its widest circumference. This is done in between two stitches, and not into a stitch, as done in the Wrapped Stitches section of this book. The pattern will tell you how to work these two stitches you have made on the next row, although in rare cases, like the Loco Shawl (page 77), they are not worked at all.

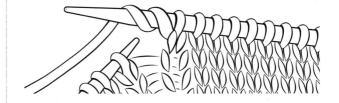

HOW TO READ CHARTS

Personally, I prefer reading knitting charts over following written directions. A chart is a visual representation of my knitting and is much easier for me to understand than a jumble of words. Other knitters won't touch a knitting chart with a ten-foot pole! I provide both charts and written instructions for almost every pattern that needs them, so if you have been eager to learn chart reading, now is your chance! If you get lost, remember that you can compare the written word to the chart.

Each square on a chart represents a stitch. You'll read across each line of the chart, performing the action denoted in that square. Every chart has a chart key telling you what the symbols in that chart mean. If you run into a gray square, this means "no stitch" and you'll skip over the square.

Single-sided lace, worked flat: If lace stitches are only worked on the right side (RS) rows of the work, only the odd-numbered rows are shown with their row numbers on the right-hand side of the chart, which will be read from right to left. There will be directions to work the wrong side (WS) rows underneath the chart.

Double-sided lace, worked flat: If lace stitches are worked on both the RS and WS rows of the work you'll see the odd-numbered row numbers on the right side of the chart, and the even-numbered row numbers on the left side. Read the odd-numbered (RS) rows from right to left, and the even-numbered (WS) rows from left to right. In this example, the chart key indicates that a blank square is a knit stitch on a RS row, and a purl stitch on a WS row, as you are turning your work and working the pattern on both sides.

Lace worked in the round: If the pattern is worked in the round, all the numbers will be on the left side of the chart and you'll work every round from right to left. This is exactly how you work your knitting, correct? From the right to the left!

Read from right to left

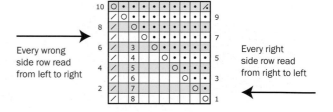

Row 2 and all even number rows (WS): K2, purl to last 2 sts, k2.

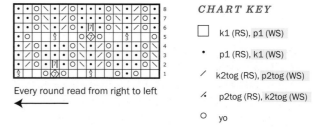

Every wrong side row read from left to right

Every right side row read from right to left

This example is highlighted and annotated for chart reading ease. See page 49.

Every round read from right to left

CHART KEY

☐ k1 (RS), p1 (WS)

• p1 (RS), k1 (WS)

╱ k2tog (RS), p2tog (WS)

╱ p2tog (RS), k2tog (WS)

○ yo

LIFELINES

Lifelines are like insurance policies for lace knitting: You won't necessarily need them, but if you run into trouble you'll be glad you invested in one! A lifeline is a smooth piece of scrap yarn, typically a lighter gauge than the yarn you are working with, in a contrasting dye-fast color that is threaded through all the live stitches on the needles. If you find a mistake and need to undo multiple rows of knitting, you can rip back to the lifeline and pick up the stitches from the scrap yarn to try again.

Placing a Lifeline

Thread a smooth piece of scrap yarn (unwaxed dental floss or buttonhole thread works well, too), onto a bent-tip tapestry needle, then thread the needle through each stitch of your knitting. If you are knitting single-sided lace, work the yarn through a plain (WS) row. Place the lifeline at the end of a repeat or on a row you know you have worked correctly, so that if you need to rip back more than a row or two you'll know you are on track. Remember to mark which row your lifeline is placed on so you know exactly where you are ripping back to.

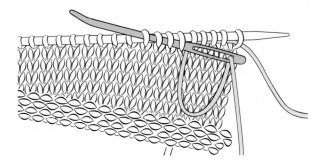

Ripping Back to a Lifeline

Remove the needle from your work. (I know, this is scary!) Slowly wind the yarn back onto its ball and stop when you reach the stitches held on the lifeline. Then, with a needle one to two sizes *smaller* than the needle you are knitting with, put the stitches onto the needle, making sure that the right leg of the stitch is to the front of your needle and the left leg is to the back. (It is *much* easier to pick up stitches with a smaller needle.) Then transfer the stitches to the working needle.

To remove a lifeline, gently pull the thread out stitch by stitch.

CHART READING TIPS AND TRICKS

» Mark up your chart so it's easier to read. For the double-sided lace chart (opposite, middle row), I highlighted all the wrong-side rows and their directions in the chart key in yellow. This way I know that a white blank box is a knit stitch, and a yellow blank box is a purl stitch. I also wrote in the stitch count of the stockinette portion so that I don't have to count each stitch individually.

» Try removable highlighter tape (available at many knitting stores and online) to keep track of the row you are on. Magnetic boards, sold for both knitting and cross-stitch, also work. (Just don't let the kids get hold of them while you are in the middle of a project—they think these boards are toys!)

» Place Post-it notes above the line you are reading to block off all the rows that you have yet to work. It will help you compare the chart to the stitches on your needles.

» Pick up a copy of JC Briar's book *Chart Reading Made Simple,* an in-depth reference on the subject.

» Remember that many charted stitches in this book are written out. If you get confused, consult the written instructions to decode the chart.

This lacy little cuff packs many of the techniques from this chapter into a small package. You'll learn right- and left-leaning single and double decreases, a centered double decrease, and yarn overs galore. The stitch count changes over the repeat, making it a learning tool to quickly master the advanced lace techniques you'll be using in other projects.

≫ Think of this design as your gateway drug to lace. Once you conquer the pattern, you'll want to make tons more . . . then see what else you can do with your mad new lace-knitting skills.

GATEWAY CUFF

Skill Level
Advanced Beginner

Materials
- 20 yd (18m) laceweight yarn
- 2 US size 2 (2.75mm) double-pointed needles, or size needed to obtain gauge
- Scrap lace yarn in contrasting color
- Tapestry needle

Yarn Used
Sweet Georgia *CashSilk Lace;* 55% silk, 45% cashmere; 1¾ oz (50g), 400 yd (366m); 1 skein in Ginger

Gauge
30 stitches and 40 rows = 4" (10cm) in stockinette stitch, blocked
43 stitches and 34 rows = 4" (10cm) in pattern stitch, blocked

Size
Small (Medium, Large)
Shown in Small
The pattern is written for multiple lengths. Instructions are given for size small, with larger sizes in parentheses.

Finished Measurements
1¾" (4.5cm) wide x 5½ (6½, 7½)" (14 [16.5, 19]cm) around

Note
- The Gateway Stitch is charted and written out; you get to decide which you prefer to work. If you read from the chart, remember that the odd-numbered rows are read from right to left and even-numbered rows from left to right as the cuff is worked flat.

CUFF

Using the long-tail cast-on method, (page 138), cast on 19 sts leaving a 10" (25.5cm) tail. Knit 1 row.

Work Rows 1–8 of the Gateway stitch from the chart or written instructions 6 (7, 8) times.

Shaping the End

ROW 1 (RS): K2, ssk, k4, s2kpo, k4, k2tog, k2—15 sts.

ROW 2 (WS): K1, purl to last st, k1.

ROW 3: K2, ssk, k2, s2kpo, k2, k2tog, k2—11 sts.

ROW 4: Repeat Row 2.

ROW 5: K2, ssk, k3, k2tog, k2—9 sts.

ROW 6: Repeat Row 2.

ROW 7: K2, ssk, k1, k2tog, k2—7 sts.

ROW 8: Repeat Row 2.

Knit 2 rows. Bind off, leaving a 10" (25.5cm) tail.

Wet-block to shape (page 140). Cuff will be approximately 6½ (7½, 8½)" (16.5 [19, 21.5]cm) long after blocking.

NOTE: Blocking is necessary so the lace can open up and lie flat!

With the RS facing up overlap ends so the cast-on edge overlaps the bound-off edge by 1" (2.5cm). Use the cast-on tail to sew the cast-on edge down. Then flip inside out and use the bind-off tail to sew down the bound-off edge at the inside of the work.

GATEWAY STITCH WRITTEN INSTRUCTIONS
(starts and ends with 19 sts)

ROW 1 (RS): K2, yo, k1, ssk, k1, k2tog, k1, p1, k1, ssk, k1, k2tog, k1, yo, k2—17 sts.

ROW 2 (WS): K1, [p7, k1] twice.

ROW 3: K2, yo, k1, yo, ssk, k1, k2tog, p1, ssk, k1, k2tog, yo, k1, yo, k2.

ROW 4: Repeat Row 2.

ROW 5: K2, yo, k3, yo, sl1k2togpo, p1, k3tog, yo, k3, yo, k2.

ROW 6: Repeat Row 2.

ROW 7: K2, yo, k5, yo, s2kpo, yo, k5, yo, k2—19 sts.

ROW 8: K1, p17, k1.

GATEWAY STITCH CHART AND KEY
(starts and ends with 19 sts)

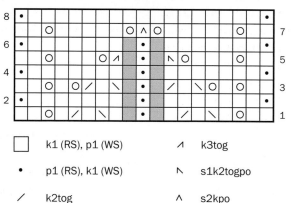

	k1 (RS), p1 (WS)	⅄	k3tog
•	p1 (RS), k1 (WS)	⋏	s1k2togpo
/	k2tog	∧	s2kpo
\	ssk	▨	no stitch
O	yo		

The Juego Cowl is worked flat, in a stitch pattern that just flies off the needles, and then it's joined together in a circle. You'll play with slipped stitches that are carried over four rows of a simple lace stitch to create this textural, mosaic-inspired fabric. If the stitch challenges you, start small with one repeat of the chart. Once you get the hang of it, cast on for the whole shebang!

» Based on a stitch developed for my Juego Mystery Shawl, Juego Cowl plays with a contrasting solid color and a hand-dyed yarn with long color repeats. I'll confess to feeding my family hummus and frozen pizza while I was knitting this design because I just had to get to the pink . . . Once you cast on Juego, you'll understand!

JUEGO COWL

Skill Level

Intermediate

Materials

- 155 yd (142m) solid-colored sport-weight yarn (color S) [2]
- 255 yd (234m) multicolored sport-weight yarn (color M) [2]
- Three US size 7 (4.5mm) needles, or size needed to obtain gauge
- Size 7 (4.5mm) crochet hook
- Scrap yarn
- Tapestry needle
- Cable needle (optional)

Yarn Used

Elsebeth Lavold *Silky Wool;* 45% wool, 35% silk, 20% nylon; 1¾ oz (50g), 192 yd (176m); 1 skein in color 54 (color S)
Noro *Silk Garden Sock;* 40% lambswool, 25% silk, 25% nylon, 10% kid mohair; 3½ oz (100g), 328 yd (300m); 1 skein in color 304 (color M)

Gauge

20 stitches and 26 rows = 4" (10cm) in stockinette stitch, in M, blocked
23 stitches and 26 rows = 4" (10cm) in pattern, blocked

Finished Measurements

Approximately 42" (106.5cm) around x 9½" (24cm) width

Notes

- The stitch for this pattern is both charted and written out. If you read from the chart, remember that the odd-numbered rows are read from right to left, and the even-numbered rows from left to right, as the cowl is worked flat.

- On right side (RS) rows, slip stitch purlwise with yarn in back.

- On wrong side (WS) rows, slip stitch purlwise with yarn in front.

Special Stitches

C1/2F

With Cable Needle: Slip the next st on the left-hand needle onto a cable needle and hold in front of work, k2, then knit stitch from the cable needle.

Without Cable Needle: Slip the right-hand needle into the back of the second and third sts on the left-hand needle, then slip the first, second, and third sts off the left-hand needle, and replace the first slipped st onto the left-hand needle, then place the 2 held sts on the right-hand needle back onto the left-hand needle. Then knit these 3 sts. What this does is exchange the positions of these 3 sts so the first st becomes the third st on the left-hand needle!

C1/2B

With Cable Needle: Slip the next 2 sts on left-hand needle onto a cable needle and hold in the back of the work, k1, then knit sts from cable needle.

Without Cable Needle: Slip the right-hand needle into the front of the third st on the left-hand needle, then slip the first, second, and third sts off the left-hand needle, and replace the first 2 slipped sts onto the left-hand needle, then place the st held on the right-hand needle onto the left-hand needle. Then knit these 3 sts. What this does is exchange the positions of these 3 sts so the third st becomes the first st on the left-hand needle!

COWL

PROVISIONAL CAST-ON: Using the crochet cast-on method (page 139) and scrap yarn, cast on 56 sts, then single crochet a few extra stitches. Cut yarn, leaving a 6" (15cm) tail, pull through last crochet stitch, and tie a knot.

SETUP ROW (WS): With color S, knit 1 row.

Body

Work Rows 1–12 of the Juego Stitch 22 times from chart or written instructions, then work Rows 1–11 once more.

If you're working from the chart, work to the blue box, repeat blue box 3 times across, and complete the chart as written. Cut color M, leaving a 6" (15cm) tail. *Do not cut color S.*

Thread live sts onto scrap yarn and wet-block (page 140) rectangle to approximately 42" (106.5cm) long x 9½" (24cm) wide. Remove the scrap yarn from the provisional cast-on and return sts to a needle; return live sts to a second needle. With right sides held together and needles parallel to each other, join together with a 3-needle bind-off (page 140) with color S. Weave in ends.

JUEGO STITCH CHART

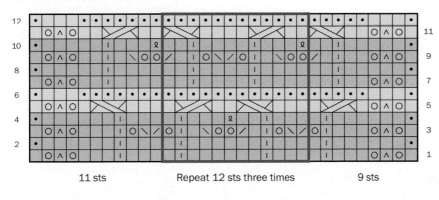

11 sts   Repeat 12 sts three times   9 sts

CHART KEY

▨ work with col S	• p1 (RS), k1 (WS)	I sl1 (see notes)	O yo
▨ work with col M	⊠ C1/2B	＼ ssk	ℓ p1tbl
☐ k1 (RS), p1 (WS)	⊠ C1/2F	／ k2tog	∧ s2kpo

JUEGO STITCH WRITTEN INSTRUCTIONS

ROW 1 (RS, WITH COLOR M): K1, yo, s2kpo, yo, k3, sl1, k1, [k3, sl1, k6, sl1, k1] 3 times, k3, sl1, k3, yo, s2kpo, yo, k1.

ROW 2 (WS, WITH COLOR M): K1, p6, sl1, p3, [p1, sl1, p6, sl1, p3] three times, p1, sl1, p6, k1.

ROW 3 (WITH COLOR M): K1, yo, s2kpo, yo, k3, sl1, yo, [k2tog, ssk, yo, sl1, k1, k2tog, yo twice, ssk, k1, sl1, yo] 3 times, k2tog, ssk, yo, sl1, k3, yo, s2kpo, yo, k1.

ROW 4 (WITH COLOR M): K1, p6, sl1, p3, [p1, sl1, p3, p1tbl, p2, sl1, p3] 3 times, p1, sl1, p6, k1.

ROW 5 (WITH COLOR S): K1, yo, s2kpo, yo, k1, C1/2B, k1, [k3, C1/2F, k2, C1/2B, k1] 3 times, k3, C1/2F, k1, yo, s2kpo, yo, k1.

ROW 6 (WITH COLOR S): K1, p3, knit to last 4 sts, p3, k1.

ROW 7 (WITH COLOR M): K1, yo, s2kpo, yo, k2, sl1, k2, [k4, sl1, k4, sl1, k2] 3 times, k4, sl1, k2, yo, s2kpo, yo, k1.

ROW 8 (WITH COLOR M): K1, p5, sl1, p4, [p2, sl1, p4, sl1, p4] 3 times, p2, sl1, p5, k1.

ROW 9 (WITH COLOR M): K1, yo, s2kpo, yo, k2, sl1, k1, k2tog, [yo twice, ssk, k1, sl1, yo, k2tog, ssk, yo, sl1, k1, k2tog] 3 times, yo twice, ssk, k1, sl1, k2, yo, s2kpo, yo, k1.

ROW 10 (WITH COLOR M): K1, p5, sl1, p3, p1tbl, [p2, sl1, p4, sl1, p3, p1tbl] 3 times, p2, sl1, p5, k1.

ROW 11 (WITH COLOR S): K1, yo, s2kpo, yo, k2, C1/2F, [k2, C1/2B, k4, C1/2F] 3 times, k2, C1/2B, k2, yo, s2kpo, yo, k1.

ROW 12 (WITH COLOR S): Repeat Row 6.

Worked from the bottom in an aran-weight yarn, this design has a sixteen-row lace border that flows into a distinctive ribbed short-row-shaped shawlette. Thicker-gauge yarn is unexpected and inviting in lace knitting. Best of all, it's fast!

» This pattern sparked some fun debate in my professional world as my tech editor and I discussed the merits of saying, "Knit the knits and purl the purls" on Twitter. Here's the secret to following these instructions: If the stitch facing you is "flat" then you should knit it; if it has a bump, then it's time to purl. Practice on some basic (nonlace) ribbing if that helps the concept "click."

FORNIDO SHAWLETTE

Skill Level
Intermediate

Materials
- 370 yd (340m) aran-weight yarn (4)
- US size 8 (5mm) circular needle, 36" (91cm) or longer, or size needed to obtain gauge
- Size H-8 (5mm) crochet hook
- 19 stitch markers
- Tapestry needle

Yarn Used
Sweet Georgia Yarn *Merino Silk Aran*; 50% merino wool, 50% silk; 3½ oz (100g), 185 yd (170m); 2 skeins in Blackberry

Gauge
14 stitches and 24 rows = 4" (10cm) in stockinette stitch, blocked
15 stitches and 24 rows = 4" (10cm) in shawl body ribbing, blocked

Finished Measurements
Approximately 47" (119cm) wide across top edge x 13" (33cm) tall at center

Note
- The stitch for this pattern is both charted and written out; you get to decide which you prefer to work. If you work from the chart, remember that the odd-numbered rows are read from right to left, and the even-numbered rows from left to right, as you are working the shawl flat.

SHAWL

Bottom Border

Using the knitted-on method (page 139), cast on 591 stitches loosely. (You can use a larger needle if this helps you keep the cast-on loose.)

If you want to work with markers, which I recommend, place them as follows:

Cast on 26 sts, place marker, *cast on 30 sts, place marker; rep from * 17 times more, cast on 25 sts—591 sts.

Begin the bottom border as follows:

Work Rows 1–16 of the Fornido Stitch from the chart or written instructions—197 sts remain.

If you are working from the chart, work the center repeat 18 times across.

If you are using markers:

On Rows 3, 5, 7, and 13, a double decrease occurs over the marker and you will need to move the marker over 1 stitch to the right as follows:

Work to 1 stitch before the marker, slip the next stitch purlwise onto the right-hand needle, remove marker, slip stitch back to the left-hand needle, place marker onto the right-hand needle, then continue as written.

Short-Row Body in Fat Rib Stitch

NOTE: If the stitch facing you is "flat," then knit it; if it has a bump, then purl.

ROW 1: K1, then work in pattern (knitting the knits and purling the purls) for 108 more sts, turn work—109 sts total. This should position you 1 st after the 11th marker.

From this point on, feel free to remove markers as you pass them.

ROW 2: Work in pattern for 21 sts, turn.

ROW 3: Work in pattern to 1 stitch before turn (there will be an obvious gap), ssk, work 2 sts in pattern, turn—1 st decreased.

ROW 4: Work in pattern to 1 stitch before turn, p2tog, work 2 sts in pattern, turn—1 st decreased.

ROW 5: Work in pattern to 1 stitch before turn, p2togtbl, work 2 sts in pattern, turn—1 st decreased.

ROW 6: Work in pattern to 1 stitch before turn, k2tog, work 2 sts in pattern, turn—1 st decreased.

ROW 7: Repeat Row 5.

ROW 8: Repeat Row 6.

ROW 9: Repeat Row 3.

ROW 10: Repeat Row 4.

ROW 11: Repeat Row 5.

ROW 12: Repeat Row 6.

ROW 13: Repeat Row 3.

ROW 14: Repeat Row 4.

ROW 15: Repeat Row 3.

ROW 16: Repeat Row 4.

ROW 17: Repeat Row 3.

ROW 18: Repeat Row 4.

ROW 19: Repeat Row 3.

ROW 20: Repeat Row 4.

ROW 21: Repeat Row 5.

ROW 22: Repeat Row 6.

ROW 23-42: Repeat Rows 3–22.

ROW 43-58: Repeat Rows 3–18.

ROW 59: Repeat Row 5.

ROW 60: Repeat Row 6.

ROW 61: Work in pattern to the last 2 sts, p2togtbl.

ROW 62: Work in pattern to the last 2 sts, k2tog—137 sts.

ROW 63: K1, work in pattern to end of row.

Lace bind-off in pattern (page 139). Weave in all ends and block (page 140).

FORNIDO STITCH CHART

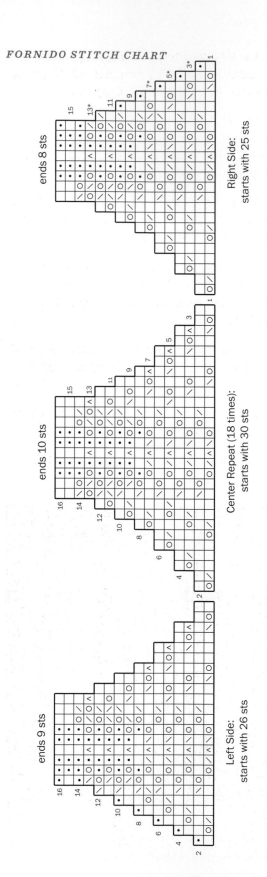

ends 8 sts

15   13*   11   9   7*   5*   3*   1

Right Side:
starts with 25 sts

ends 10 sts

15   13   11   9   7   5   3   1

16   14   12   10   8   6   4   2

Center Repeat (18 times):
starts with 30 sts

ends 9 sts

15   13   11   9   7   5   3

16   14   12   10   8   6   4   2

Left Side:
starts with 26 sts

* See pattern for notes about markers on these rows.

CHART KEY

	k1 (RS), p1 (WS)
•	p1 (RS), k1 (WS)
/	k2tog (RS), p2tog (WS)
\	ssk (RS), p2togtbl (WS)
∧	s2kpo
O	yo

FORNIDO STITCH WRITTEN INSTRUCTIONS

ROW 1 (RS): K1, yo, ssk, k4, yo, ssk, s2kpo, k2tog, yo, k4, k2tog, yo, k3, k2tog, yo, [k1, (yo, ssk, k3) twice, k1, yo, ssk, s2kpo, k2tog, yo, k1, (k3, k2tog, yo) twice] 18 times, k1, (yo, ssk, k3) twice, k1, yo, ssk, s2kpo, k2tog, yo, k4, k2tog, yo, k1—551 sts.

ROW 2 (WS): K1, p4, p2togtbl, yo, p5, yo, p2tog, p10, [p9, p2togtbl, yo, p5, yo, p2tog, p10] 18 times, p9, p2togtbl, yo, p5, yo, p2tog, p4, k1.

ROW 3: K1, yo, ssk, k3, yo, ssk, s2kpo, k2tog, yo, k3, k2tog, yo, k2, k2tog, yo, [s2kpo, (yo, ssk, k2) twice, k1, yo, ssk, s2kpo, k2tog, yo, k1, (k2, k2tog, yo) twice] 18 times, s2kpo, (yo, ssk, k2) twice, k1, yo, ssk, s2kpo, k2tog, yo, k3, k2tog, yo, k1—473 sts.

ROW 4: K1, p3, p2togtbl, yo, p5, yo, p2tog, p8, [p7, p2togtbl, yo, p5, yo, p2tog, p8] 18 times, p7, p2togtbl, yo, p5, yo, p2tog, p3, k1.

ROW 5: K1, yo, ssk, k2, yo, ssk, s2kpo, k2tog, yo, k2, k2tog, yo, k1, k2tog, yo, [s2kpo, (yo, ssk, k1) twice, k1, yo, ssk, s2kpo, k2tog, yo, k1, (k1, k2tog, yo) twice] 18 times, s2kpo, (yo, ssk, k1) twice, k1, yo, ssk, s2kpo, k2tog, yo, k2, k2tog, yo, k1—395 sts.

ROW 6: K1, p2, p2togtbl, yo, p5, yo, p2tog, p6, [p5, p2togtbl, yo, p5, yo, p2tog, p6] 18 times, p5, p2togtbl, yo, p5, yo, p2tog, p2, k1.

ROW 7: [K1, yo, ssk] twice, s2kpo, k2tog, yo, k3, k2tog, yo, [s2kpo, yo, ssk, k3, yo, ssk, s2kpo, k2tog, yo, k3, k2tog, yo] 18 times, s2kpo, yo, ssk, k3, yo, ssk, s2kpo, [k2tog, yo, k1] twice—317 sts.

ROW 8: K1, p1, p2togtbl, yo, k1, p3, k1, yo, p2tog, p4, [p3, p2togtbl, yo, k1, p3, k1, yo, p2tog, p4] 18 times, p3, p2togtbl, yo, k1, p3, k1, yo, p2tog, p1, k1.

ROW 9: K2, k2tog, yo, p1, s2kpo, p1, yo, ssk, k1, k2tog, yo, [k1, yo, ssk, k1, k2tog, yo, p1, s2kpo, p1, yo, ssk, k1, k2tog, yo] 18 times, k1, yo, ssk, k1, k2tog, yo, p1, s2kpo, p1, yo, ssk, k2—277 sts.

ROW 10: K1, p2togtbl, yo, k2, p1, k2, yo, p2tog, p3, [p2, p2togtbl, yo, k2, p1, k2, yo, p2tog, p3] 18 times, p2, p2togtbl, yo, k2, p1, k2, yo, p2tog, k1.

ROW 11: K1, k2tog, yo, p1, s2kpo, p1, yo, ssk, k2tog, yo, [k1, yo, ssk, k2tog, yo, p1, s2kpo, p1, yo, ssk, k2tog, yo] 18 times, k1, yo, ssk, k2tog, yo, p1, s2kpo, p1, yo, ssk, k1—237 sts.

ROW 12: P2togtbl, yo, k2, p1, k2, yo, p2tog, p2, [p1, p2togtbl, yo, k2, p1, k2, yo, p2tog, p2] 18 times, p1, p2togtbl, yo, k2, p1, k2, yo, p2tog.

ROW 13: K2tog, yo, p1, s2kpo, p1, yo, ssk, yo, [s2kpo, yo, k2tog, yo, p1, s2kpo, p1, yo, ssk, yo] 18 times, s2kpo, yo, k2tog, yo, p1, s2kpo, p1, yo, ssk—197 sts.

ROW 14: K3, p1, k2, yo, p2tog, p1, [p2togtbl, yo, k2, p1, k2, yo, p2tog, p1] 18 times, p2togtbl, yo, k2, p1, k3.

ROW 15: K1, p2, k1, p2, k2, [k3, p2, k1, p2, k2] 18 times, k3, p2, k1, p2, k1.

ROW 16: K3, p1, k2, p3, [p2, k2, p1, k2, p3] 18 times, p2, k2, p1, k3.

Worked in two halves and joined together at the top of the hood, Techo will become one of your favorite winter accessories. The fabric is a combination of double-sided lace with intricate ribbing, and an integrated I-cord edging. The pattern repeats allow you to keep track of your knitting without the use of stitch markers.

» This design started with the yarn. I'd been ogling Galler's Prime Alpaca hanks at my LYS forever, with a one-skein project in mind. I knew that it could be big, but because of the yarn's high alpaca content the design needed to have enough structure that it wouldn't droop!

TECHO HOODED SCARF

Skill level
Intermediate

Materials
- 560 yd (512m) sport-weight yarn ⓶
- US size 6 (4mm) circular needle, 24" (60cm) or longer, or size needed to obtain gauge
- Scrap yarn or extra needle
- Tapestry needle
- Stitch markers (optional)

Yarn Used
Galler *Heather Prime Alpaca;* 100% superfine alpaca; 8 oz (226g), 665 yd (608m); 1 skein in color 213

Gauge
20 stitches and 24 rows = 4" (10cm) in stockinette stitch, blocked

Finished Measurements
8" (20.5cm) wide x 35" (89cm) long (from hem of scarf to top of hood), blocked

Notes
- On every row the first three stitches are knit and the last three stitches are slipped purlwise one at a time with yarn in front. This creates the integrated I-cord edging.

- The stitches are both charted and written out. If you're working from the chart, remember that the odd-numbered rows are read from right to left, and the even-numbered rows from left to right, to work the scarf flat.

- Markers can be placed to delineate each lace repeat, or use the purl stitches between each lace motif as markers.

LEFT HALF

Using the long-tail method (page 138), cast on 56 sts.

SETUP ROW (WS): Knit to last 3 sts, slip last 3 sts purlwise with yarn in front.

ROW 1 (RS): K3, work Row 1 of Lace Ribbing Stitch twice, p1, work Row 1 of Leaf Stitch, k1, p1, slip last 3 sts purlwise with yarn in front.

ROW 2 (WS): K4, p1, work Row 2 of Leaf Stitch, k1, work Row 2 of Lace Ribbing Stitch twice, slip last 3 sts purlwise with yarn in front.

Continue as established working from charts or written instructions through Row 10, then repeat Rows 1–10 twelve times more, place stitches onto on a spare needle or scrap yarn. Cut yarn leaving a 6" (15cm) tail.

RIGHT HALF

Using the long-tail method (page 138), cast on 56 sts.

SETUP ROW (WS): Knit to last 3 sts, slip last 3 sts purlwise with yarn in front.

ROW 1 (RS): K3, p1, k1, work Row 1 of Leaf Stitch, work Row 1 of Lace Ribbing Stitch twice, p1, slip last 3 sts purlwise with yarn in front.

ROW 2 (WS): K4, work Row 2 of Lace Ribbing Stitch twice, work Row 2 of Leaf Stitch, p1, k1, slip last 3 sts purlwise with yarn in front.

Continue as established working from charts or written instructions through Row 10, then repeat Rows 1–10 twelve times more. *Do not cut yarn.*

JOIN HALVES FOR HOOD

ROW 1 (RS): K3, p1, k1, work Row 1 of Leaf Stitch, work Row 1 of Lace Ribbing Stitch twice, p1, k2tog, p1, then working across held sts for Left Half, p1, k2tog, work Row 1 of Lace Ribbing Stitch twice, p1, work Row 1 of Leaf Stitch, k1, p1, slip last 3 sts purlwise with yarn in front—106 sts.

ROW 2 (WS): K4, p1, work Row 2 of Leaf Stitch, k1, work Row 2 of Lace Ribbing Stitch twice, p1, k2tog, p1, k1, work Row 2 of Lace Ribbing Stitch twice, work Row 2 of Leaf Stitch, p1, k1 slip last 3 sts purlwise with yarn in front—105 sts.

ROW 3: K3, p1, k1, work Row 3 of Leaf Stitch, work Row 3 of Lace Ribbing Stitch twice, [p1, k1] twice, work Row 3 of Lace Ribbing Stitch twice, p1, work Row 3 of Leaf Stitch, k1, p1, slip last 3 sts purlwise with yarn in front.

ROW 4: K4, p1, work Row 4 of Leaf Stitch, k1, work Row 4 of Lace Ribbing Stitch twice, [p1, k1] twice, work Row 4 of Lace Ribbing Stitch twice, work Row 4 of Leaf Stitch, p1, k1, slip last 3 sts purlwise with yarn in front.

Continue as established working from charts or written instructions through Row 10, then repeat Rows 1–10 six times more.

Work Rows 1–9 once more, then work final row as follows:

FINAL ROW (WS): K4, p1, work Row 10 of Leaf Stitch, k1, work Row 10 of Lace Ribbing Stitch twice, p1, p2tog, k1, work Row 10 of Lace Ribbing Stitch twice, work Row 10 of Leaf Stitch, p1, k1, slip last 3 sts purlwise with yarn in front—108 sts.

Cut yarn leaving a 45" (114cm) tail.

FINISHING

Separate sts to distribute an even number on 2 needles. Hold both halves of the hood with wrong sides together and using Kitchener stitch (page 138), graft the two pieces together.

Weave in ends and block (page 140).

NOTE: The scarf will become much longer with blocking.

Optional Tassel

Cut twenty-one 12" (30.5cm) strands of yarn.

Lay 20 of the strands down flat and tie the 21st strand tightly around the midpoint. Lift with the tie to fold strands in half. Then with a separate 24" (61cm) long strand of yarn wrap about 1" (2.5cm) down from tied midpoint and weave in ends and fasten off. Attach with tie to the top back of the hood.

LEAF STITCH WRITTEN INSTRUCTIONS
(begins and ends with 15 sts)

ROW 1 (RS): Yo, k1, k2tog, p1, ssk, k1, p1, k1, k2tog, p1, ssk, k1, yo—13 sts.

ROW 2 (WS): P6, k1, p6.

ROW 3: Yo, k1, yo, k2tog, p1, ssk, p1, k2tog, p1, ssk, yo, k1, yo.

ROW 4: Repeat Row 2.

ROW 5: Yo, k3, yo, sl1k2togpo, p1, k3tog, yo, k3, yo.

ROW 6: Purl across.

ROW 7: Yo, k5, yo, s2kpo, yo, k5, yo—15 sts.

ROW 8: Purl across.

ROW 9: Yo, k1, k2tog, p1, ssk, k1, yo, p1, yo, k1, k2tog, p1, ssk, k1, yo.

ROW 10: P7, k1, p7.

LACE RIBBING STITCH WRITTEN INSTRUCTIONS
(16 sts)

ROW 1 (RS): P1, k2tog, k1, p1, yo twice, k2, s2kpo, k2, yo twice, p1, k1, ssk.

ROW 2 (WS): P3, k1, p7, k1, p3, k1.

ROWS 3, 5, 7, AND 9: Repeat Row 1.

ROWS 4, 6, 8, AND 10: Repeat Row 2.

LEAF STITCH CHART
(begins and ends with 15 sts)

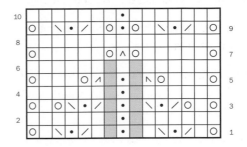

LACE RIBBING STITCH CHART (16 sts)

CHART KEY

☐ k1 (RS), p1 (WS)		⋏ sl1k2togpo
• p1 (RS), k1 (WS)		⋌ k3tog
╱ k2tog		O yo
╲ ssk		⋀ s2kpo
▨ no stitch		

This lace rectangle can be worn as a scarf if left unbuttoned, or you can button each arm into a cylinder to create a shrug. Worked from the center out, you'll first knit a square of double-sided lace in the round for the back. Then each "arm" is created by working a flat lace panel from the center. It's simple shaping, but gives dramatic, convertible, and wearable results!

» I have a bit of an obsession with lace designs that grow from the center out. The trouble is, this method creates a square or a circle, but this time I wanted a rectangle. I sketched, swatched, then pondered. I decided to work a lace square, and then riff off the stitch pattern on opposite sides to turn my square into a rectangle. It is so gratifying when my ideas actually work!

QUADRO CONVERTIBLE SHRUG

Skill level
Advanced Intermediate

Materials
- 600 (680, 750) yd (549 [622, 686]m) sport-weight yarn (2)

Needles for Square
- US size 6 (4mm) double-pointed needles (or 1 long circular needle), or size needed to obtain gauge

Needles for Square and Arms
- US size 6 (4mm) 16" (40cm) circular needle, or size needed to obtain gauge
- US size 6 (4mm) 24" (60cm) circular needle, or size needed to obtain gauge
- US size 6 (4mm) 32" (80cm) or 36" (90cm) circular needle, or size needed to obtain gauge

Needles for Edging
- US size 6 (4mm) double-pointed needles, or size needed to obtain gauge
- US size 6 (4mm) 40" (100cm) circular needle, or size needed to obtain gauge

- Stitch markers
- Tapestry needle
- Eight 1" (2.5cm) diameter buttons
- Sewing needle and coordinated thread

Yarn Used
Blue Sky Alpaca *Alpaca Silk;* 50% alpaca, 50% silk; 1¾ oz (50g), 146 yd (134m); 5 (5, 6) skeins in Sapphire

Gauge
22 stitches and 30 rows = 4" (10cm) in stockinette stitch, blocked

Size
Small (Medium, Large)
Shown in Small
The pattern is written for multiple lengths. Instructions are for size small, with larger sizes in parentheses.

Finished Measurements

Approximately 18" (45.5cm) wide at center back x 12½" (32cm) wide at arm x 54 (58, 62)" (137 [147, 157.5]cm) from wrist to wrist

Notes

• All the stitches in this pattern are charted. For a cheat sheet with the written instructions, visit www.nelkinde-signs.com/quadro.

• Remember that the Quadro *Square* Stitch is worked in the round, so read every round from right to left. The Quadro *Flat* Stitch is worked flat, so the odd-numbered rows are read from right to left, and the even-numbered rows from left to right.

Special Stitch

Make 7

Into the same stitch, (k1, yo) 3 times, k1. This turns 1 stitch into 7 sts.

BEGIN SQUARE

Using the circular method (page 139), cast on 4 sts.

Slide sts to the other end of the needle and purl 1 row distributing sts evenly over needles as preferred. Join for working in the round, being careful not to twist the sts. If desired, mark the beginning of the round with a removable stitch marker or safety pin.

Begin working from the Quadro Square Stitch Chart; you will be repeating the chart four times around.

Work Rounds 1–44 once—57 sts in each repeat; 228 sts total.

NOTE: If you are working on double-pointed needles, switch to the circular needle when sts get too crowded, placing st markers to divide the sts from each needle. Use a different color marker for the start of the round. As the stitches get crowded on that cord, switch to longer ones. If you own a set of inter-changeable needles, this is a great time to use them!

SETUP FOR LEFT ARM

Place the last 57 sts of the round just worked onto a long piece of scrap yarn (Right Arm).

K57, place these sts onto a second long piece of scrap yarn (Top).

Work Row 1 of the Quadro Transition Stitch from the chart once—57 sts (Left Arm).

Place the next 57 sts onto a third piece of scrap yarn (Bottom).

Turn. You will now be working flat on the Left Arm.

Work Rows 2–8 from the Quadro Transition Stitch, from the chart.

Work Rows 1–8 of Quadro Flat Stitch using the chart 15 (17, 19) times.

FINAL ROW (RS): K1, p2, k10, p1, k29, p1, k10, p2, k1.

Lace bind-off (page 140) in pattern.

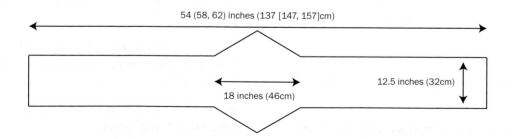

54 (58, 62) inches (137 [147, 157]cm)

12.5 inches (32cm)

18 inches (46cm)

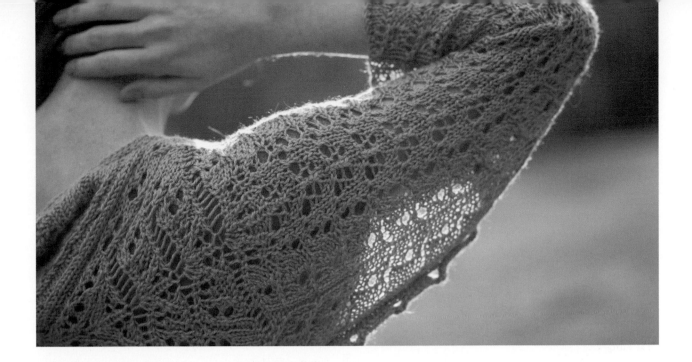

RIGHT ARM

With RS facing, place 57 sts for Bottom onto a needle.

Rejoin yarn at the start of the Bottom and k57.

Replace these sts onto the third long piece of scrap yarn (Bottom).

Place the held 57 stitches for the Right Arm back onto the needle.

Begin with Row 1 of Quadro Transition Stitch on these 57 sts and work as for Left Arm.

TOP EDGE

With RS facing and starting at upper right-hand corner of the Right Arm with the longest needle, pick up and knit 128 (142, 160) sts along the top of the Right Arm. When you reach the live 57 sts on the scrap yarn, place them onto a needle and knit across them, then pick up and knit 128 (142, 160) sts along the top of the Left Arm, to the end—313 (341, 376) sts.

Turn work.

Using the backwards loop method (page 139), cast on 3 sts.

With the double-pointed needles begin to work the attached I-cord as follows:

*K2, sl1 knitwise; k1 live st from shrug, pass slipped st over st just knit. *Do not turn work.*

Slip 3 sts just worked back to left-hand needle and bring yarn around the back of the work, ready to begin working next row.

Rep from * until all live sts are worked.

Work a twisted attached I-cord as follows:

NOTE: This will create buttonhole loops and edging at the same time.

Turn work, so RS is facing. You will be working across the top edge of the shawl one last time.

***ROW 1**: K2, sl1, pick up and knit 1 st tbl from top of I-cord edge just worked, pass slipped st over st just knit. *Do not turn.*

ROWS 2-6: K2, sl1; pick up and knit 1 st from top of I-cord edge just worked, pass slipped st over st just knit. *Do not turn.*

ROW 7: K2, sl1, pick up and knit 1 st tbl from top of I-cord edge just worked, pass slipped st over st just knit. *Do not turn.*

ROWS 8-11: K3, slide sts to the other end of the needle (unattached I-cord).

Twist double-pointed needle all the way around clockwise (360°), making sure working yarn ends up at the back of the work.

Skip 2 stitches on the I-cord edge and repeat from * across, end with row 7, k3tog.

Cut yarn leaving a 6" (15cm) tail, pull yarn through the last stitch to bind off.

BOTTOM EDGE

With RS facing and starting at the lower left-hand corner of the Left Side, work edging as you did for the Top Edge.

FINISHING

Weave in all ends and block (page 140).

With WS held together, fold sleeve in half so the Top Edge overlaps the bottom one, then sew on 4 buttons opposite every other loop, starting at the loop closest to the end of the sleeve. Repeat on the other sleeve.

QUADRO TRANSITION STITCH (57 sts)

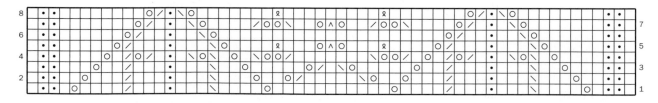

QUADRO FLAT STITCH (57 sts)

QUADRO SQUARE STITCH

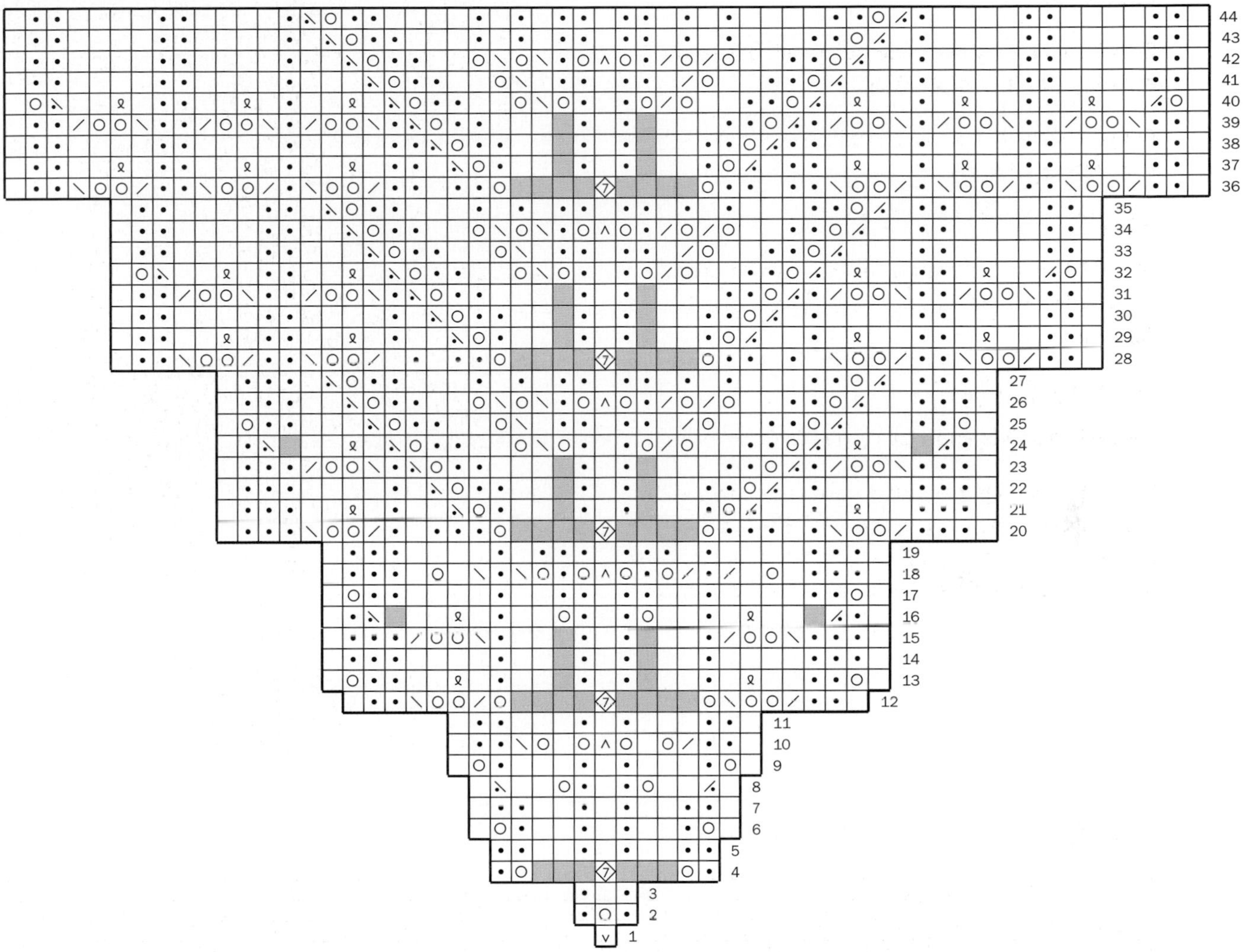

CHART KEY

- □ knit (RS) purl (WS)
- • purl (RS) knit (WS)
- / k2tog (RS) p2tog (WS)
- \ ssk (RS) p2togtbl (WS)
- O yo
- ℓ k1tbl (RS) p1tbl (WS)
- [grey square] no stitch
- [diamond with 7] make 7 (see notes)
- ∧ s2kpo
- /· p2tog (RS), k2tog (WS)
- \· p2togtbl (RS), ssk (WS)
- v pfb

Worked from the top down in the round, this lacy tam has textural nupps and lace stitches worked on every round. The brim is finished off with an elastic bind-off that might become your new favorite way to bind off in pattern!

» Lace doilies don't fit my home's decor, but I inherited a box-full from my grandma and love to pull them out and study the crochet stitches. I realized if I designed a lacy tam from the top down it would be a similar concept, but knit. What fun to turn this passion into a new hat!

GYRUS TAM

Skill level
Advanced Intermediate

Materials
- 190 yd (173m) fingering-weight yarn
  [1]
- Set of 5 US size 4 (3.5mm) double-pointed needles (or 1 long circular needle), or size needed to obtain gauge
- US size 4 (3.5mm) 16" (40cm) circular needle, or size needed to obtain gauge
- US size 3 (3.25mm) 16" (40cm) circular needle, or size needed to obtain gauge
- Tapestry needle

Yarn Used
Shibui *Staccato*; 70% superwash merino wool, 30% silk; 1¾ oz (50g), 191 yd (175m); 1 skein in Fjord

Gauge
24 stitches and 32 rows = 4" (10cm) in stockinette stitch on larger needles, blocked
16 stitches and 20 rounds = 4" (10cm) in Lace Stitch on larger needles, blocked

Size
To fit an average adult head

Finished Measurements
18" (45.5cm) unstretched band circumference x 7" (18cm) deep

Notes
- The stitch in this pattern is both charted and written out. If you work from the chart, remember that since you are working in the round you read every round from right to left.
- If you're using stitch markers to separate repeats, you will need to move them over by one stitch on Rounds 7 and 12 of the Crown Increase Chart and Rounds 1 and 9 of the Tam Body Chart as the double decrease at the end of the repeat is worked over the marker.

Special Stitches
Make 7
Into the same stitch, (k1, yo) 3 times, k1.
This takes 1 stitch and makes it 7 sts, or a nupp. A nupp is simply a concentration of stitches that are increased and decreased over 2 rows.
7to1 (decreasing nupp)
Sl4 sts one at a time knitwise, k3tog, pass 4 slipped stitches over.

TOP

Using the circular method (page 139), and with the larger needle, cast on 8 sts.

Slide sts to the other end of the needle and knit 1 row distributing sts evenly over needles as preferred. Join for working in the round, being careful not to twist the sts. If desired, mark the beginning of the round with a removable stitch marker or safety pin.

SETUP ROUND: *K1f&b three times, k1; rep from * once more—14 sts.

Remove the end-of-round marker, knit 1 st and replace end-of-round marker.

If you're working with double-pointed needles, distribute sts evenly over the needles.

CROWN INCREASES

Begin working from the Crown Increase Chart or written instructions. You will be repeating the chart 7 times each round.

Work Rounds 1–23 once—112 sts total.

AT THE BEGINNING OF ROUNDS 7 AND 12: Remove the end-of-round marker, knit 1 st and replace the end-of-round marker.

NOTE: If you're working on double-pointed needles, when your sts get too crowded on the needles switch to the same size circular needle, placing st markers to divide up the sts for each repeat. Use a different color marker for the start of the round.

BODY

Work Rounds 1–16 of Tam Body Chart or written instructions once. You will be repeating the chart 7 times each round.

AT THE BEGINNING OF ROUNDS 1 AND 9: Remove the end-of-round marker, knit one st, and replace end-of-round marker.

Then work Rounds 1–12 once more, following directions for marker on Rounds 1 and 9 as before.

DECREASE FOR RIBBING

Switch to smaller needles.

DECREASE ROUND: *K2, p2tog, p1, k2, p1; rep from * to end of round—98 sts.

RIBBING ROUND: *K2, p2, k2, p1; rep from * to end of round.

Repeat Ribbing Round 8 more times.

Lace bind-off in pattern (page 140). Weave in ends and block (page 140).

CROWN INCREASE WRITTEN INSTRUCTIONS
(starts with 2 sts, ends with 16 sts)

Worked 7 times each round.

ROUNDS 1 AND 2: P1, k1—2 sts.

ROUND 3: Yo, p1, yo, k1—4 sts.

ROUND 4: K1, p1, k2.

ROUND 5: P3, k1.

ROUND 6: Yo, p3, yo, k1—6 sts.

ROUND 7: Yo, p3, yo, s2kpo.

ROUND 8: Yo, k1, p3tog, k1, yo, k1.

ROUND 9: P1, yo, k1, p1, k1, yo, p2—8 sts.

ROUNDS 10 AND 11: P1, yo, k2tog, p1, ssk, yo, p2.

ROUND 12: Yo, k2, yo, make 7, yo, k2, yo, p3tog—10 sts.

ROUND 13: P1, ssk, yo, p1, 7to1, p1, yo, k2tog, p2.

ROUNDS 14 AND 15: P1, ssk, yo, p3, yo, k2tog, p2.

ROUND 16: Yo, make 7, yo, k2, p3tog, k2, [yo, p1] twice—12 sts.

ROUND 17: P1, 7to1, p1, yo, k2tog, p1, ssk, yo, p4.

ROUND 18: Yo, p3, yo, k2tog, p1, ssk, yo, p3, yo, p1—14 sts.

ROUND 19: K1, p3, yo, k2tog, p1, ssk, yo, p3, k1, p1.

ROUND 20: Yo, k1, p3tog, k2, yo, p1, yo, k2, p3tog, k1, yo, make 7.

ROUND 21: P1, yo, k1, p1, ssk, yo, p3, yo, k2tog, p1, k1, yo, p1, 7to1—16 sts.

ROUNDS 22 AND 23: P1, yo, k2tog, p1, ssk, yo, p3, yo, k2tog, p1, ssk, yo, p2.

TAM BODY WRITTEN INSTRUCTIONS
(16-st repeat)

Worked 7 times each round.

ROUND 1: K2, yo, p1, yo, k2, p3tog, k2, yo, make 7, yo, k2, p3tog.

ROUND 2: Ssk, yo, p3, yo, k2tog, p1, ssk, yo, p1, 7to1, p1, yo, k2tog, p1.

ROUNDS 3 AND 4: [Ssk, yo, p3, yo, k2tog, p1] twice.

ROUND 5: Yo, k2, p3tog, k2, yo, make 7, yo, k2, p3tog, k2, yo, p1.

ROUND 6: P1, yo, k2tog, p1, ssk, yo, p1, 7to1, p1, yo, k2tog, p1, ssk, yo, p2.

ROUNDS 7 AND 8: [P1, yo, k2tog, p1, ssk, yo, p2] twice.

ROUND 9: K2, yo, make 7, yo, k2, p3tog, k2, yo, p1, yo, k2, p3tog.

ROUND 10: Ssk, yo, p1, 7to1, p1, yo, k2tog, p1, ssk, yo, p3, yo, k2tog, p1.

ROUNDS 11 AND 12: Repeat Row 3.

ROUND 13: Yo, k2, p3tog, k2, yo, p1, yo, k2, p3tog, k2, yo, make 7.

ROUND 14: P1, yo, k2tog, p1, ssk, yo, p3, yo, k2tog, p1, ssk, yo, p1, 7to1.

ROUNDS 15 AND 16: Repeat Round 7.

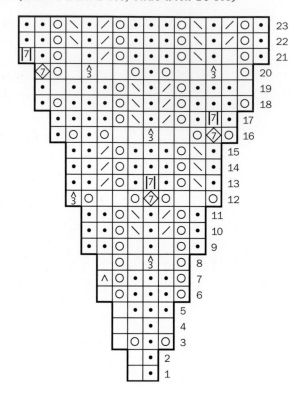

CROWN INCREASE CHART
(starts with 2 sts, ends with 16 sts)

TAM BODY CHART (16 st repeat)

CHART KEY

☐	k1	∧	s2kpo
•	p1	⅜	purl 3 together
/	k2tog	○	yo
\	ssk	◇7	make 7 (see notes)
7⎮	7to1 (see notes)		

A top-down lace shawl, Loco starts with two increasing triangles framing a center panel. Multiple charts and double-sided lace keep the knitting interesting. Knitting this shawl is a true labor of love, and the finished piece will be an heirloom to enjoy for many years to come.

≫ The Loco Stitch originated in a German stitch dictionary, but by the time I translated the written instructions and charts (quite different from what we are used to) I had something entirely new, and a little bit crazy. The design started with this stitch offset in the center panel and on each edge, and blossomed from there. Designing on the needles is one of my favorite ways to explore a new knitting concept, and working on Loco Shawl did not disappoint!

LOCO SHAWL

Skill level
Advanced

Materials
• 910 yd (832m) laceweight yarn
  (0)
• US size 5 (3.75mm) needles, or size needed to obtain gauge
• Stitch markers, 4 color A, 18 color B
• Tapestry needle

Yarn Used
Swan's Island *Natural Colors Merino Silk;* 50% merino wool, 50% silk; 1¾ oz (50g), 550 yd (503m); 2 skeins in Apricot

Gauge
20 stitches and 32 rows = 4" (10cm) in stockinette stitch, blocked

Finished Measurements
72" (183cm) across at top x 23½" (59.5cm) deep at center back

Notes
• Double Yarn Overs: In this pattern the double yarn overs are worked on one row, and then dropped on the next row. When you reach a double yarn over from a previous row, *drop it* before continuing the row. These double yarn overs are not included in the stitch counts as they are not considered stitches.

• Increase counts noted at the end of rows are for extra stitches incorporated into each edge of the Right and Left Triangle. The Loco Stitch and its variations change in count from row to row. This is reflected on the chart and in the written instructions for each stitch but *not* at the end of each row.

Special Stitches
Loco-7
Drop both yarn overs from the left-hand needle, then with working yarn *in front* bring the right-hand needle *to the back* of the work and reach down 7 rows, stick the needle through from back to front, yarn over needle, and pull through to the back of the work. This "catches" the 7 double yarn overs worked in the previous rows and gathers them together into a bundle. You are working a purl stitch, but 7 rows down.

Poco Loco

With working yarn *in front,* bring the right-hand needle *to the back* of the work and reach down 1 row, stick the needle through from back to front between stitches, yarn over needle and pull through to the back of the work. This "catches" the running yarn from the previous row. You are making a purl stitch, but 1 row down.

SHAWL

Using the long-tail method (page 138), cast on 83 sts.

SETUP ROW (WS): K17 (Left Edge), place marker A, k3 (Left Triangle), place marker A, k43 (Center Panel), place marker A, k3 (Right Triangle), place marker A, k17 (Right Edge).

SECTION 1

NOTE: You will be increasing the stockinette stitch triangles on each side of the Center Panel.

Work from the chart or the written instructions as follows:

ROW 1 (RS): K1, work Row 1 of Loco Stitch, sl marker, p1, yo, k1, yo, p1, sl marker, work Row 1 of Loco Center Panel, sl marker, p1, yo, k1, yo, p1, sl marker, work Row 1 of Loco Stitch, k1—4 sts increased, 2 in each triangle.

ROW 2 (WS): K1, work Row 2 of Loco Stitch, sl marker, k1, p3, k1, sl marker, work Row 2 of Loco Center Panel, sl marker, k1, p3, k1, sl marker, work Row 2 of Loco Stitch, k1.

ROW 3: K1, work Row 3 of Loco Stitch, sl marker, p1, yo, knit to 1 st before marker, yo, p1, sl marker, work Row 3 of Loco Center Panel, sl marker, p1, yo, knit to 1 st before marker, yo, p1, sl marker, work Row 3 of Loco Stitch, k1—4 sts increased, 2 in each triangle.

ROW 4: K1, work Row 4 of Loco Stitch, sl marker, k1, purl to 1 st before marker, k1, sl marker, work Row 4 of Loco Center Panel, sl marker, k1, purl to 1 st before marker, k1, sl marker, work Row 4 of Loco Stitch, k1.

Continue as established working Rows 1–10 of Loco Stitch and Loco Center Panel once, then work Rows 1–10 of Loco Stitch 7 times more and Rows 11–20 of Loco Center Panel 7 times more—242 sts; 17 sts (Right Edge), 83 sts (Right Triangle), 42 sts (Center Panel), 83 sts (Left Triangle), 17 sts (Left Edge).

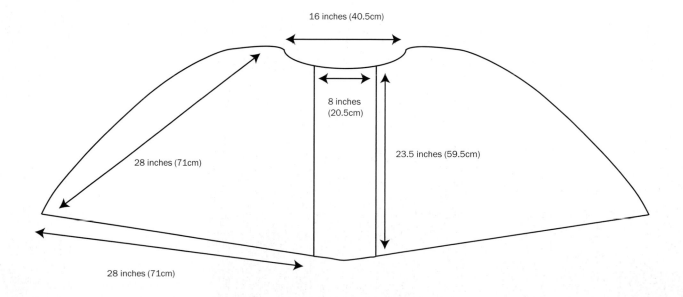

16 inches (40.5cm)

8 inches (20.5cm)

23.5 inches (59.5cm)

28 inches (71cm)

28 inches (71cm)

SECTION 2

NOTES

- You will be integrating a modified Loco Stitch into the stockinette stitch triangles on each side of the Center Panel, which you will continue working in pattern as established.

- Slip all markers as you reach them. I have included some markers in these directions, to help you keep track of the sections.

ROW 1 (RS): K1, work Row 1 of Loco Stitch, sl marker A, p1, yo, k2, m1R, k1, place marker B, work Row 1 of Poco Loco Stitch, place marker B, knit to 1 st before next marker, yo, p1, sl marker A, work Row 11 of Loco Center Panel, sl marker A, p1, yo, knit to 20 sts before next marker, place marker B, work Row 1 of Poco Loco Stitch, place marker B, k1, m1L, k2, yo, p1, sl marker A, work Row 1 of Loco Stitch, k1—6 sts increased (3 sts in Right and Left Triangles).

ROW 2 (WS): K1, work Row 2 of Loco Stitch, sl marker A, k1, purl to next marker, sl marker B, work Row 2 of Poco Loco Stitch, sl marker B, purl to 1 st before next marker, k1, sl marker A, work Row 12 of Loco Center Panel, sl marker A, k1, purl to next marker, sl marker B, work Row 2 of Poco Loco Stitch, sl marker B, purl to 1 st before last marker, k1, sl marker A, work Row 2 of Loco Stitch, k1.

ROW 3: K1, work Row 3 of Loco Stitch, sl marker A, p1, yo, knit to next marker, sl marker B, work Row 3 of Poco Loco Stitch, sl marker B, knit to 1 st before next marker, yo, p1, sl marker A, work Row 13 of Loco Center Panel, sl marker A, p1, yo, knit to next marker, sl marker B, work Row 3 of Poco Loco Stitch, sl marker B, knit to 1 st before next marker, yo, p1, sl marker A, work Row 3 of Loco Stitch, k1—4 sts increased (2 sts in Right and Left Triangles).

ROW 4: Repeat Row 2, but working next row in stitch patterns.

ROW 5: K1, work Row 5 of Loco Stitch, sl marker A, p1, yo, k2, m1R, knit to the next marker, sl marker B, work Row 5 of Poco Loco Stitch, sl marker B, knit to 1 st before next marker, yo, p1, sl marker A, work Row 15 of Loco Center Panel, sl marker A, p1, yo, knit to

next marker, sl marker B, work Row 5 of Poco Loco Stitch, sl marker B, knit to 3 sts before next marker, m1L, k2, yo, p1, sl marker A, work Row 5 of Loco Stitch, k1—6 sts increased (3 sts in Right and Left Triangles).

ROW 6: Repeat Row 2, working next row in stitch patterns.

ROW 7: Repeat Row 3, working next row in stitch patterns—4 sts increased (2 sts in Right and Left Triangles).

ROW 8: Repeat Row 2, working next row in stitch patterns.

ROW 9: Repeat Row 5, working next row in stitch patterns—6 sts increased (3 sts in Right and Left Triangles).

ROW 10: Repeat Row 2, working next row in stitch patterns.

ROW 11: K1, work Row 1 of Loco Stitch, sl marker A, p1, yo, k2, m1R, knit to next marker, sl marker B, work Row 1 of Poco Loco Stitch twice, place marker B, knit to 1 st before next marker, yo, p1, sl marker A, work Row 11 of Loco Center Panel, sl marker A, p1, yo, knit to 16 sts before next marker, place marker B, work Row 1 of Poco Loco Stitch twice, sl marker B, knit to 3 sts before next marker, m1L, k2, yo, p1, sl marker A, work Row 1 of Loco Stitch, k1—6 sts increased (3 sts in Right and Left Triangles).

ROWS 12-20: Repeat Rows 2–10 working 2 repeats of the Poco Loco Stitch—20 sts increased (10 sts in Right and Left Triangles).

ROW 21: K1, work Row 1 of Loco Stitch, sl marker A, p1, yo, k2, m1R, k1, place marker B, work Row 1 of Poco Loco Stitch 4 times, place marker B, knit to 1 st before the next marker, yo, p1, sl marker A, work Row 11 of Loco Center Panel, sl marker A, p1, yo, knit to 16 sts before the next marker, place marker B, work Row 1 of Poco Loco Stitch 4 times, place marker B, k1, m1L, k2, yo, p1, sl marker A, work Row 1 of Loco Stitch, k1—6 sts increased (3 sts in Right and Left Triangles).

ROWS 22-30: Repeat Rows 2–10 working 4 repeats of the Poco Loco Stitch—20 sts increased (10 sts in Right and Left Triangles).

ROW 31: Work as for Row 11, working 5 repeats of the Poco Loco Stitch—6 sts increased (3 sts in Right and Left Triangles).

ROWS 32-40: Repeat Rows 2–10 working 5 repeats of the Poco Loco Stitch—20 sts increased (10 sts in Right and Left Triangles).

ROW 41: Repeat Row 21, working 7 repeats of the Poco Loco Stitch—6 sts increased (3 sts in Right and Left Triangles).

ROWS 42-50: Repeat Rows 2–10 working 7 repeats of the Poco Loco Stitch—20 sts increased (10 sts in Right and Left Triangles).

ROW 51: K1, work Row 1 of Loco Stitch, sl marker A, p1, yo, knit to next marker, sl marker B, work Row 1 of Poco Loco Stitch 8 times, place marker B, knit to 3 sts before next marker, m1R, k2, yo, p1, sl marker A, work Row 11 of Loco Center Panel, sl marker A, p1, yo, k2, m1L, knit to 16 sts before next marker, place marker B, work Row 1 of Poco Loco Stitch 8 times, sl marker B, knit to 1 st before next marker, yo, p1, sl marker A, work Row 1 of Loco Stitch, k1—6 sts increased (3 sts in Right and Left Triangles).

ROWS 52-54: Repeat Rows 2–4, working 8 repeats of the Poco Loco Stitch—4 sts increased (2 sts in Right and Left Triangles).

ROW 55: K1, work Row 5 of Loco Stitch, sl marker A, p1, yo, knit to next marker, sl marker B, work Row 5 of Poco Loco Stitch 8 times, sl marker B, knit to 3 sts before next marker, m1R, k2, yo, p1, sl marker A, work Row 15 of Loco Center Panel, sl marker A, p1, yo, k2, m1L, knit to next marker, sl marker B, work Row 5 of Poco Loco Stitch 8 times, sl marker B, knit to 1 st before next marker, yo, p1, sl marker A, work Row 5 of Loco Stitch, k1—6 sts increased (3 sts in Right and Left Triangles).

ROWS 56-58: Repeat Rows 2–4, working next row in stitch patterns and 8 repeats of the Poco Loco Stitch—4 sts increased (2 sts in Right and Left Triangles).

ROW 59: K1, work Row 9 of Loco Stitch, sl marker A, p1, knit to next marker, sl marker B, work Row 9 of Poco Loco Stitch 8 times, sl marker B, knit to 3 sts before next marker, m1R, k2, yo, p1, sl marker A, work Row 19 of Loco Center Panel, sl marker A, p1, yo, k2, m1L, knit to next marker, sl marker B, work Row 9 of Poco Loco Stitch 8 times, sl marker B, knit to 1 st before next marker, p1, sl marker A, work Row 9 of Loco Stitch, k1—4 sts increased—396 sts; 17 sts (Right Edge), 160 sts (Right Triangle), 42 sts (Center Panel), 160 sts (Left Triangle), 17 sts (Left Edge).

ROW 60: Repeat Row 2, working next row in stitch patterns and 8 repeats of the Poco Loco Stitch.

ROW 61: K1, work Row 1 of Loco Stitch, sl marker A, work Row 1 of Poco Loco Stitch 10 times, sl marker A, work Row 11 of Loco Center Panel, sl marker A, work Row 1 of Poco Loco Stitch 10 times, sl marker A, work Row 1 of Loco Stitch, k1.

ROW 62: K1, work Row 2 of Loco Stitch, sl marker A, work Row 2 of Poco Loco Stitch 10 times, sl marker A, work Row 12 of Loco Center Panel, sl marker A, work Row 2 of Poco Loco Stitch 10 times, sl marker A, work Row 2 of Loco Stitch, k1.

ROWS 63-70: Continue in pattern as established, without working increases.

ROW 71: K1, work Row 1 of Loco Stitch 11 times, sl marker A, work Row 11 of Center Panel, sl marker A, work Row 1 of Loco Stitch 11 times, k1.

ROWS 72-76: Repeat Row 71, but work next row in stitch patterns.

ROW 77: K1, work Row 7 of Loco Stitch 12 times, k16, work Row 7 of Loco Stitch 12 times, k1.

ROW 78: K1, work Row 8 of Loco Stitch 12 times, p16, work Row 8 of Loco Stitch 12 times, k1.

ROWS 79 AND 80: Repeat Rows 77 and 78, working next row in stitch patterns—402 sts.

SECTION 3 *(edging)*

ROW 1 (RS): K1, work Row 1 of Loco Edging 25 times, k1—452sts.

ROWS 2-10: Repeat Row 1, working next row in stitch pattern—752 sts when Loco Edging is complete.

Lace bind-off (page 140) in pattern. Weave in all ends and block (page 140).

LOCO STITCH WRITTEN INSTRUCTIONS

(starts and ends with 16 sts)

NOTE: See pattern notes (page 77) about double yarn overs.

ROW 1 (RS): P1, yo, k5, k2tog, double yo, ssk, k5, yo, p1—16 sts.

ROW 2 (WS): K1, p5, p2togtbl, double yo, p2tog, p5, k1—14 sts.

ROW 3: P1, yo, s2kpo, yo, k1, k2tog, double yo, ssk, k1, yo, s2kpo, yo, p1—12 sts.

ROW 4: K1, p3, p2togtbl, double yo, p2tog, p3, k1—10 sts.

ROW 5: P1, yo, k2tog twice, double yo, ssk twice, yo, p1—8 sts.

ROW 6: K1, p1, p2togtbl, double yo, p2tog, p1, k1—6 sts.

ROW 7: P1, k2tog, double yo, ssk, p1—4 sts.

ROW 8: K1, p1, Loco-7, p1, k1—5 sts.

ROW 9: P1, k1, backwards loop cast on 5 sts, k1f&b, backwards loop cast on 5 sts, k1, p1—16 sts.

ROW 10: K1, p14, k1—16 sts.

LOCO STITCH CHART
(starts and ends with 16 sts)

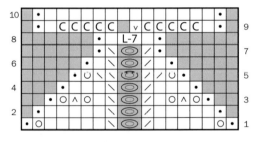

LOCO CENTER PANEL STITCH CHART
(starts with 43 sts, ends with 42 sts)

CHART KEY

	k1 (RS), p1 (WS)	\	ssk (RS), p2togtbl (WS)	C	backwards loop cast-on
•	p1 (RS), k1 (WS)	⬭	double yarn over (see pattern notes, page 77)	L-7	Loco-7
O	yo	^	s2kpo	PL	Poco Loco
/	k2tog (RS), p2tog (WS)	v	k1f&b		no stitch

LOCO CENTER PANEL STITCH WRITTEN INSTRUCTIONS

(starts with 43 sts, ends with 42 sts)

NOTE: See pattern notes (page 87) about double yarn overs.

ROW 1 (RS): P1, yo, k5, k2tog, double yo, ssk, k5, yo, p2, k2, k2tog, k1, ssk, k2, p2, yo, k5, k2tog, double yo, ssk, k5, yo, p1—41 sts.

ROW 2 (WS): K1, p5, p2togtbl, double yo, p2tog, p5, k2, p1, p2togtbl, p1, p2tog, p1, k2, p5, p2togtbl, double yo, p2tog, p5, k1—35 sts.

ROW 3: P1, yo, s2kpo, yo, k1, ktog, double yo, ssk, k1, yo, s2kpo, yo, p2, k2tog, k1, ssk, p2, yo, s2kpo, yo, k1, k2tog, double yo, ssk, k1, yo, s2kpo, yo, p1—29 sts.

ROW 4: K1, p3, p2togtbl, double yo, p2tog, p3, [k2, p3] twice, p2togtbl, double yo, p2tog, p3, k1—25 sts.

ROW 5: P1, yo, k2tog twice, double yo, ssk twice. yo, p2, k1, backwards loop cast on 5 sts, k1f&b, backwards loop cast on 5 sts, k1, p2, yo, k2tog twice, double yo, ssk twice, yo, p1—32 sts.

ROW 6: K1, p1, p2togtbl, double yo, p2tog, p1, k2, p14, k2, p1, p2togtbl, double yo, p2tog, p1, k1—28 sts.

ROW 7: P1, k2tog, double yo, ssk, p2, yo, k5, k2tog, double yo, ssk, k5, yo, p2, k2tog, double yo, ssk, p1—24 sts.

ROW 8: K1, p1, Loco-7, p1, k2, p5, p2togtbl, double yo, p2tog, p5, k2, p1, Loco-7, p1, k1—24 sts.

ROW 9: P1, k1, backwards loop cast on 5 sts, k1f&b, backwards loop cast on 5 sts, k1, p2, yo, s2kpo, yo, k1, k2tog, double yo, ssk, k1, yo, s2kpo, yo, p2, k1, backwards loop cast on 5 sts, k1f&b, backwards loop cast on 5 sts, k1, p2—44 sts.

POCO LOCO STITCH CHART
(starts and ends with 16 sts)

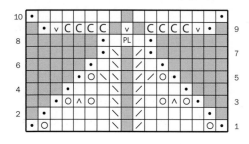

LOCO EDGING STITCH CHART
(starts with 16 sts, ends with 30 sts)

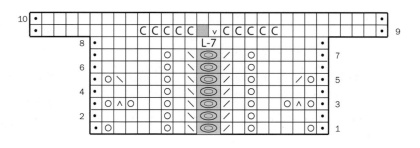

CHART KEY

☐ k1 (RS), p1 (WS)	\ ssk (RS), p2togtbl (WS)	C backwards loop cast-on
• p1 (RS), k1 (WS)	⬯ double yarn over (see pattern notes, page 77)	L-7 Loco-7
O yo	∧ s2kpo	PL Poco Loco
/ k2tog (RS), p2tog (WS)	v k1f&b	no stitch

ROW 10: K1, p14, k2, p3, p2togtbl, double yo, p2tog, p3, k2, p14, k1—42 sts.

ROW 11: P1, yo, k5, k2tog, double yo, ssk, k5, yo, p2, yo, k2tog twice, double yo, ssk twice, yo, p2, yo, k5, k2tog, double yo, ssk, k5, yo, p1—40 sts.

ROW 12: K1, p5, p2togtbl, double yo, p2tog, p5, k2, p1, p2togtbl, double yo, p2tog, p1, k2, p5, p2togtbl, double yo, p2tog, p5, k1—34 sts.

ROW 13: P1, yo, s2kpo, yo, k1, k2tog, double yo, ssk, k1, yo, s2kpo, yo, p2, k2tog, double yo, ssk, p2, yo, s2kpo, yo, k1, k2tog, double yo, ssk, k1, yo, s2kpo, yo, p1—28 sts.

ROW 14: K1, p3, p2togtbl, double yo, p2tog, p3, k2, p1, Loco-7, p1, k2, p3, p2togtbl, double yo, p2tog, p3, k1—25 sts.

ROW 15: Repeat Row 5.

ROW 16: Repeat Row 6.

ROW 17: Repeat Row 7.

ROW 18: Repeat Row 8.

ROW 19: Repeat Row 9.

ROW 20: Repeat Row 10.

POCO LOCO STITCH WRITTEN INSTRUCTIONS

(starts and ends with 16 sts)

ROW 1 (RS): P1, yo, k5, k2tog, ssk, k5, yo, p1—16 sts.

ROW 2 (WS): K1, p5, p2togtbl, p2tog, p5, k1—14 sts.

ROW 3: P1, yo, s2kpo, yo, k1, k2tog, ssk, k1, yo, s2kpo, yo, p1—12 sts.

ROW 4: K1, p3, p2togtbl, p2tog, p3, k1—10 sts.

ROW 5: P1, yo, k2tog twice, ssk twice, yo, p1—8 sts.

ROW 6: K1, p1, p2togtbl, p2tog, p1, k1—6 sts.

ROW 7: P1, k2tog, ssk, p1—4 sts.

ROW 8: K1, p1, Poco Loco, p1, k1—5 sts.

ROW 9: P1, [k1f&b, backwards loop cast on 4 sts] twice, k1f&b, p1—16 sts.

ROW 10: K1, p14, k1—16 sts.

LOCO EDGING WRITTEN INSTRUCTIONS

(starts with 16 sts, ends with 30 sts)

NOTE: See pattern notes (page 87) about double yo.

ROW 1 (RS): P1, yo, k4, yo, k1, k2tog, double yo, ssk, k1, yo, k4, yo, p1—18 sts.

ROW 2 (WS): K1, p5, yo, p1, p2togtbl, double yo, p2tog, p1, yo, p5, k1.

ROW 3: P1, yo, s2kpo, yo, k2, yo, k1, k2tog, double yo, ssk, k1, yo, k2, yo, s2kpo, yo, p1.

ROW 4: Repeat Row 2.

ROW 5: P1, yo, k2tog, k3, yo, k1, k2tog, double yo, ssk, k1, yo, k3, ssk, yo, p1.

ROW 6: Repeat Row 2.

ROW 7: P1, k5, yo, k1, k2tog, double yo, ssk, k1, yo, k5, p1.

ROW 8: K1, p8, Loco-7, p8, k1—19 sts.

ROW 9: P1, k8, backwards loop cast on 5 sts, k1f&b, backwards loop cast on 5 sts, k8, p1—30 sts.

ROW 10: K1, p28, k1.

beaded
BEAUTIES

When I first learned how to knit, it didn't occur to me that beads could be incorporated into knitting. I had made a lot of peyote-stitch jewelry as a teenager and had abandoned my beading box years before. One day, when I was developing a lace stitch, I started to wonder what it would look like if there were beads floating on the yarn overs. I swatched and ripped, then swatched and ripped again—until I figured out how to get the beads to lie exactly where I wanted them to be. Then came the tricksy part: I had to figure out how I did it, and then find a way to explain it simply so others could work the pattern as well.

Now it's hard for me to look at something I have designed and not add beads to it! Sometimes the beads are prestrung on the yarn so that they float on your stitches; other times a bead is placed in order to sit on a stitch (page 91). This chapter of the book delves deeply into many techniques for knitting with beads that I have learned and developed over the last few years. You'll find a few of my signature knitted jewelry designs, as well as jaunty hats, mitts, and scarves with a smattering of sparkling beads. Expect to get as obsessed as I have. Your knitting might never be the same again.

BEADS

If you are placing beads on a stitch, feel free to choose any bead manufacturer. For prestrung projects, you need to choose beads with smooth interiors to avoid damaging the yarn as they slide down it. I buy glass Japanese seed beads for their uniformity, both inside and out. A few Japanese bead manufacturers you will run across are Toho, Miyuki, and Matsuno. I also use high-quality Czech crystal beads as accents on the Hibisco Necklace (page 99) and in other designs in my line. In the materials list, I include the manufacturer, color, and finish, when available, for the beads in each design. Use this as a guide to help kickstart your own bead creativity.

BEAD SIZE CHART

Glass Seed Beads	Beads per Gram*	Exterior Diameter	Interior Hole Diameter
Size 6/0	12	3.3mm	1.7mm
Size 8/0	40	2.5mm	1.2mm
*This is an approximate number for round seed beads. If the bead has a distinctive shape, weigh the beads to get an accurate count of beads per gram.			

All the beads I work with in this book are either size 6 or 8 glass seed beads. The most important thing to note is that size 6 beads are actually larger than size 8 beads. The larger the bead size, the smaller the bead! Beads are normally sold by the gram, so refer to the Bead Size Chart (above) to help determine the amount you need.

Most seed beads are round, but you will also find triangular-shaped seed beads (some with rounded corners, others very sharp), square beads, and cylindrical beads (also called delica). Keep in mind that within each beaded pattern I give an approximate weight for the bead shape I used. Should you substitute a different shape bead, you'll have to calculate how many grams you will need. First, weigh the beads to ascertain how many are in one gram, and then divide the total number of beads called for by that number. This tells you approximately how many beads to purchase. Remember to always buy more beads than you will need. Undoubtedly, a few will spill!

MATCHING BEADS TO YARN

Your best bet is to bring your yarn to a local bead store. The beads' color will change as you string them, and you can test the beads' size against the yarn weight. I don't have a local bead store, so when I travel I buy little tubes of different colors, shapes, and sizes of beads. Then when I am designing at home I can find the best match for a particular yarn.

I tend to choose beads that coordinate with my yarn color, as I like the beading to be a bit subtle. That said, I don't want to go through all that extra trouble if the beads are going to get lost in my knitting. For this reason I like to use beads with a metallic lining or an iridescent finish, which adds shine and sparkle. Beads come lined and unlined, with either a metallic or a color lining on a round or square interior hole. I have a special place in my bead box for square-holed, silver-lined Matsuno beads because the sharp interior corners of the hole catch the light, as seen in the Reversible Undulating Waves Scarf and the Cha-Ching Tam (pages 129 and 103). The glass may be either opaque or transparent, and may have a matte coating, or even an AB (Aurora Borealis–rainbow) finish.

Another important consideration is which size bead to use with which weight yarn. When placing beads, two strands of yarn need to fit through the hole of the bead. When prestringing beads, only one strand of the yarn must go through, so a smaller bead can be used. Always make sure the beads slide easily on the yarn. If they need to be forced down the yarn, this means the bead is too small and the yarn is potentially being damaged by the bead. If it slides all over the place, the bead is too big!

Yarn Weight	Placed Beads	Prestrung Beads
Lace	Size 6 or 8	Size 8
Light Fingering	Size 6	Size 8
Fingering/Sock	Size 6	Size 6 or 8
Sport	Size 6	Size 6
DK	Size 6	Size 6

YARN CONTENT AND BEADS

If you are working with beads that are placed on stitches, you don't need to worry as much about the yarn's fiber content and structure, but if you are working with prestrung beads, please read this information closely!

Since sliding beads down the yarn causes friction and can abrade fibers, it's important to choose a yarn that is strong and can handle this action. Yarn with multiple plies and a tight twist will stand up to the friction well. Find a yarn with a high merino wool or cotton content, and perhaps even some nylon. I shy away from yarns with more than 5–10 percent silk or cashmere, as those fragile fibers degrade easily.

I selected the materials in this section to give you a good sampling of yarns that perform beautifully with prestrung beads. The only single ply I used is in the Cha-Ching Tam because this yarn is slightly felted and quite strong. Also, since this is a cap, not mitts, and incorporates fewer beads, it holds up to the technique nicely.

The Yarn Versus Bead Test

Do you have a yarn in your stash that you'd love to use, but you aren't sure that it will hold up to beads sliding along it? Take an 8-inch (20.5cm) strand of the yarn, string ten beads, and tie it around your wrist. Wear it like this for a few days, and you will quickly know if the yarn can withstand the friction.

PRESTRUNG BEADS: TIPS AND TRICKS

» Do not thread more than approximately four hundred beads at a time, or more than the number specified in the pattern. It is not fun to move a thousand beads down the yarn at one time, or to rethread them if you run into a knot in the yarn. Plus, too many beads cause unnecessary wear and tear on the yarn.

» String the beads from the outside of the yarn ball or cake, not from inside a center-pull ball, in case you encounter yarn tangles.

» Beads can act as stitch counters. Determine how many beads you need for a row and slide them up the yarn, ready to work. If you end up with beads left over, or not enough beads, you know that row has a mistake.

» Blocking will help straighten stitches, open up lace, and tighten up decreases, which helps keep beads in their place.

» If beads are sliding all over while you knit, one of two things is happening: Either the beads are too big for the yarn or you need to go down a needle size to get a smaller gauge.

» If a bead ends up on the wrong side of a stitch or yarn over, you don't need to rip back. Just wait until you are a few rows beyond the mistake and massage it back into place.

KNITTING WITH BEADS

Beads can either be prestrung on the yarn, or placed on a single stitch. When prestrung, the bead sits horizontally between two stitches; when placed, the bead sits vertically on the stitch. I routinely use these two techniques and will teach you how to master both. Aesthetically, I prefer the way prestrung beads float, adding movement and kinetic energy to knitwear. Placing locks the beads in place for a more static effect, and works well with more fragile fibers (page 89). I've designed a few pieces that use both techniques in one project, letting you mix different bead sizes and colors.

▶ Look for this icon, indicating that you'll find a video for the technique on my website: www.nelkindesigns.com/tutorials.

Placing Beads with a Crochet Hook

▶ When working with a size 6 or larger bead, you can use a 0.75–1mm crochet hook to place the bead. Take the crochet hook and put it through the center of your bead, then slip the next stitch on the left-hand needle onto the hook, and slide the bead down onto the stitch. See page 92 for how to handle this stitch next.

Placing Beads with Super Floss

▶ If you're working with a bead smaller than size 6, use this technique as the hole is too small for the crochet hook method. Super Floss is a type of dental floss that has an integrated threader. To use it for beading, tie a knot on the "floss" end of the strand and preload it with beads.

Take the stiff end of the floss and slide into the next stitch on the left-hand needle purlwise. Fold the stiff end of the tip toward itself so it runs parallel to the floss. Slide a bead down to the tip, and then pinch both the floss and the tip so that the stitch is "sandwiched." Slip the stitch off the left-hand needle, and slide the bead down onto the stitch.

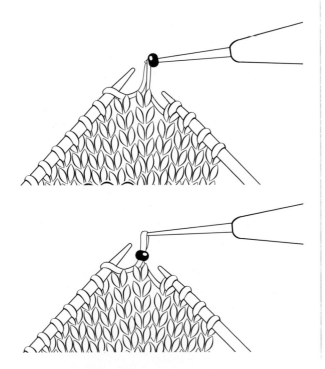

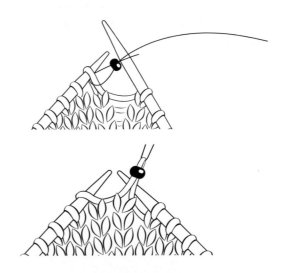

Once a Bead Is Placed

There are two choices on how to handle the stitch. The pattern will tell you which treatment is appropriate.

- Slip the stitch onto the right-hand needle purlwise without twisting it, removing the crochet hook or super floss as you do. The working yarn comes behind the bead, "pushing" it to the front of the work.

- Place the stitch back on the left-hand needle removing the crochet hook or super floss as you do, and then knit or purl it. This ensures that the bead can be seen from the front and back of the work.

Prestringing Beads

▶ With a dental floss threader or a large eye beading needle, thread the end of the yarn through the eye of the needle, then pick up beads with the needle and slide them down over the tail and onto the working yarn.

At points in the pattern it will be necessary to cut the yarn, leaving a 6-inch (15cm) tail, in order to string more beads. After the beads are strung, leave a tail (at least 6 inches [15cm] long) and work the next row. You will have a few ends to weave in when you are done!

Slipping Beads

▶ Slide the bead up the yarn to the stitch on the right-hand needle as far as it will go, and then work the next stitch. This will lock the bead between two stitches. When worked between two purl stitches on the right side (or two knit stitches on the wrong side), the bead will be pushed to the right side of the work as it is sitting on the purl bump in between the stitches.

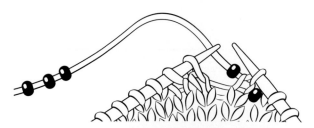

Knit or Purl with 1+ Bead(s)

Insert right-hand needle into the loop on the left-hand needle to work a stitch as usual, then slide the bead(s) up until it is almost but not quite touching the right-hand needle. Wrap the yarn around the right-hand needle, ready to make the new stitch. The bead should be sitting "on top" of the right-hand needle. Then work the stitch, pulling the bead through. The bead(s) will lock into place on the new stitch you just made.

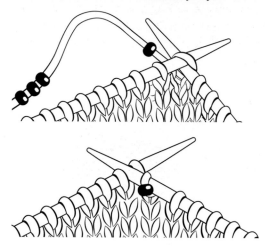

NOTE: The illustration shows this worked with a knit stitch, but it is the same for a purl stitch.

Yarn Over with 1+ Bead(s)

Slide bead(s) up the yarn so that they sit directly next to the right-hand needle. Work the yarn over, then work the following st as directed. The bead(s) will lock into place on the yarn over.

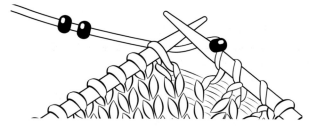

Wrapping with Bead(s)

Insert the right-hand needle into the next stitch on the left-hand needle, then slide the bead(s) up until they are almost but not quite touching the right-hand needle, wrap the yarn as indicated around the right-hand needle, at its widest circumference, and then complete the stitch as usual.

Working into a Stitch with a Bead

When you come to a stitch or yarn over from the previous row that has a bead (or multiple beads), it is important to situate the bead(s) so that they land correctly. Beads can either be to the front of the left-hand needle (on the right leg of the stitch) or to the back of the left-hand needle (on the left leg of the stitch).

This is true if you are working a single stitch or a stitch that is part of a decrease. The pattern will specify which side of the needle the bead should be on when you come to that stitch.

BEAD TO FRONT

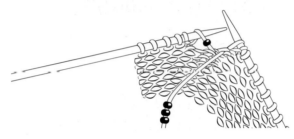

BEAD TO BACK

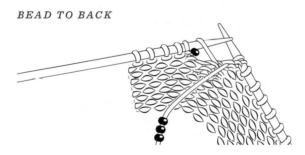

Lace Bind-Off with Beads

▶ This bind-off is the same as the Lace Bind-Off (page 140), with the addition of beads!

When the pattern asks you to incorporate a bead, work as follows:

Slide the left-hand needle into the 2 sts on the right-hand needle, then slide a bead up until it is almost touching the left-hand needle. Wrap the yarn around the left-hand needle, ready to make the new stitch. The bead should be sitting "on top" of the needle. Then work the decrease. The bead will lock into place on the new stitch.

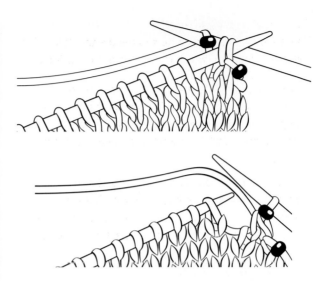

When you come to this stitch with the bead on your next bound off stitch, orient the bead as follows: If you are working a purlwise lace bind-off, it should be to the back of the needle. For a knitwise lace bind-off, it should be to the front of the needle.

A HUGE NOTE ABOUT KNITTING WITH BEADS

All these designs will be beautiful without beads! If you aren't aesthetically drawn to working with beads, or you just don't want to incorporate beads in your knitting, feel free to skip the beading instructions. Laden Fauxbius (page 117) is a great example of this option . . . I like it without beads just as much as with them!

This undulating Bulb Stitch teaches two beading techniques: slipping beads and placing beads, plus my favorite integrated I-cord edging. Use the stitch in a cuff or a necklace, or even a headband. It's easy to add more repeats should you want the piece longer or shorter.

» I'll never tire of designing simple beaded cuff stitches. I played with this puppy for hours to get it just right and loved every minute of it. One thing I learned is that it needs to be knit at a dense gauge to keep the bulb from rolling: The whole undulating effect is lost if it's not knit tightly enough.

BULB CUFF AND NECKLACE

Skill level
Advanced Beginner

Materials
For Cuff
- 12 (13, 14) yd (11 [12, 13]m) fingering-weight yarn ⓵
- 3 size 6 glass seed beads (approximately 1 gram) (B, bigger)
- 62 (70, 78) size 8 glass seed beads (approximately 2 grams) (A, smaller)

For Necklace
- 35 (39, 43) yd (32 [36, 39]m) fingering-weight yarn ⓵

- 10 (11, 12) size 6 glass seed beads (approximately 1 gram) (B, bigger)
- 216 (238, 260) size 8 glass seed beads (approximately 6 (7, 8) grams) (A, smaller)
- Sew-on snap
- Sewing needle and coordinated sewing thread

For Both
- US size 2 (2.75mm) needles, or size needed to obtain gauge
- Dental floss threader
- Super Floss or crochet hook (0.75–1mm)
- Tapestry needle

Yarn Used
For Cuff
SpaceCadet Creations *Celeste;* 100% merino wool; 3½ oz (100g), 490 yd (448m); 1 skein in Feather

For Necklace
Koigu *KPPPM;* 100% superwash merino wool; 1¾ oz (50g), 175 yd (160m), 1 skein in color 342

Beads Used

For Cuff

6/0 Miyuki seed bead, transparent lined green with an AB finish, color 344 (B)

8/0 Toho seed bead, frosted black diamond with a silver lining, color 29Af/d (A)

For Necklace

6/0 Miyuki seed bead, opaque metallic dark plum iris, color 454 (B)

8/0 Matsuno seed bead, transparent light tourmaline with a silver-lined square hole and AB finish (A)

Gauge

32 stitches and 40 rows = 4" (10cm) in stockinette stitch, blocked

36 stitches and 48 rows = 4" (10cm) in Bulb Stitch, blocked

Finished Measurements

Cuff: 5½ (6, 6½)" (14 [15, 16.5]cm) around

Necklace: 16 (17½, 19)" (40 [44.5, 48.5]cm) around

The pattern is written for multiple lengths. Instructions are given for size small, with larger sizes in parentheses.

Special Stitch

Place Bead: With Super Floss, place bead onto the next stitch on the left-hand needle, then *knit* the stitch (page 91).

CUFF

Setup

Using dental floss threader, string 62 (70, 78) size 8 beads onto yarn (see page 92).

Using the long-tail method (page 138), cast on 5 sts.

With working yarn:

ROW 1 (RS): Knit to end of row.

ROW 2 (WS): K1, m1R, k3, m1L, k1—7 sts.

ROWS 3 AND 4: Knit to end of row.

*Work Rows 1–18 of the Bulb Stitch from the chart or written instructions, then work Rows 1–2 of the Bulb Stitch from the chart or written instructions 2 (4, 6) times more; rep from * once more, then work Rows 1–18 of the Bulb Stitch once more.

Final Rows

ROWS 1 AND 2: Knit to end of row.

ROW 3: K1, ssk, k1, k2tog, k1—5 sts remain.

ROW 4: Knit to end of row.

Bind off all sts.

Finishing

Wet-block (page 140) flat, using pins to shape the bulbs. Seam ends of cuff together. Weave in ends.

NECKLACE

Setup

Using dental floss threader, string 216 (238, 260) size 8 beads onto yarn (page 92).

Using the long-tail method (page 138), cast on 7 sts.

Knit 1 row.

*Work Rows 1–18 of the Bulb Stitch from the chart or written instructions, then work Rows 1–2 of the Bulb Stitch from the chart or written instructions 2 times more; rep from * 8 (9, 10) times more, then work Rows 1–18 of the Bulb Stitch from the chart or written instructions once more.

Final Rows

Knit 8 rows.

Bind off all sts.

Finishing

Wet-block flat (page 140), using pins to shape the bulbs. Weave in ends.

With right side facing, sew 1 side of a snap centered onto the garter stitch tab. Sew the other end of the snap onto the wrong side of the second "bulb" worked. Overlap and attach to hide the garter stitch tab.

BULB STITCH CHART (over 7 sts increased to 13; 18 A beads, 1 B bead per repeat)

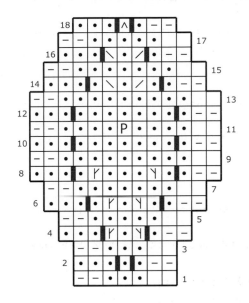

CHART KEY

☐ k1 (RS), p1 (WS)

• p1 (RS), k1 (WS)

Ɣ make 1 right

Y make 1 left

▌▐ slip bead

P place bead

╱ k2tog

╲ ssk

∧ s2kpo

– slip st purlwise with yarn in front

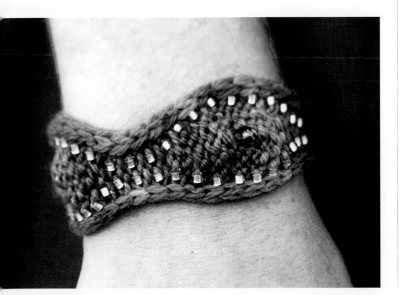

BULB STITCH WRITTEN INSTRUCTIONS

(over 7 sts increased to 13; 18 A beads, 1 B bead per repeat)

ROW 1: K2, p to last 2 sts, sl2 sts purlwise with yarn in front.

ROW 2: K3, slip 1 bead, k1, slip 1 bead, k1, sl2 sts purlwise with yarn in front.

ROW 3: Repeat Row 1.

ROW 4: K3, slip 1 bead, m1R, k1, m1L, slip 1 bead, k1, sl2 sts purlwise with yarn in front—9 sts.

ROW 5: Repeat Row 1.

ROW 6: K3, slip 1 bead, k1, m1R, k1, m1L, k1, slip 1 bead, k1, sl2 sts purlwise with yarn in front—11 sts.

ROW 7: Repeat Row 1.

ROW 8: K3, slip 1 bead, k1, m1R, k3, m1L, k1, slip 1 bead, k1, sl2 sts purlwise with yarn in front—13 sts.

ROW 9: Repeat Row 1.

ROW 10: K3, slip 1 bead, knit to last 3 sts, slip 1 bead, k1, sl2 sts purlwise with yarn in front.

ROW 11: K2, p4, place bead, purl to last 2 sts, sl2 sts purlwise with yarn in front.

ROW 12: Repeat Row 10.

ROW 13: Repeat Row 1.

ROW 14: K3, slip 1 bead, k1, ssk, k1, k2tog, k1, slip 1 bead, k1, sl2 sts purlwise with yarn in front—11 sts.

ROW 15: Repeat Row 1.

ROW 16: K3, slip 1 bead, ssk, k1, k2tog, slip 1 bead, k1, sl2 sts purlwise with yarn in front—9 sts.

ROW 17: Repeat Row 1.

ROW 18: K3, slip 1 bead, s2kpo, slip 1 bead, k1, sl2 sts purlwise with yarn in front—7 sts.

This necklace takes knitting with beads one step further by introducing the concept of prestringing beads in a predetermined order. The prestrung beads create a color pattern, while gentle ruffles develop at the neckline. The necklace is finished off with my all-time favorite lace bind-off with beads incorporated at the center.

≫ The only bad part about summer is that it's hard to "tag" yourself as a knitter! That's when knitted jewelry comes to the rescue. Knit in tencel, a cellulositic fiber that is cool to the touch, this necklace is flattering with an open neckline and lightweight dress. The beads add weight so it sits on your neck perfectly!

HIBISCO NECKLACE

Skill level
Intermediate

Materials
• 25 yd (23m) laceweight yarn 🧵
• 16 size 6 glass seed beads
  (approximately 2 grams) (B, bigger)
• 70 size 8 glass seed beads
  (approximately 2 grams) (A, smaller)
• Twenty-five 4mm Czech crystal beads
  (C, crystal)
• US size 2 (2.75mm) needles, or size
  needed to obtain gauge
• Dental floss threader
• 2 stitch markers
• Clasp of your choice
• Sewing needle and coordinated
  thread
• Tapestry needle

Yarn Used
Prism *Delicato;* 100% tencel; 4 oz
(113g), 630 yd (576m); 1 skein in
Hibiscus

Beads Used
6/0 Matsuno seed bead, transparent
amethyst with purple lining and AB
finish, color 356 (B)
8/0 Miyuki seed bead, crystal with noir
lining and AB finish, color 283 (A)
4mm Preciosa crystal bicone bead,
Bermuda Blue (C)

Gauge
25 stitches and 42 rows = 4" (10cm) in
stockinette stitch, blocked
26 stitches and 40 rows = 4" (10cm) in
k1, p1 ribbing, blocked

Finished Measurements
16 (18, 20)" around (40 [45.5, 51]cm)
The pattern is written for multiple
lengths. Instructions are given for size
small, with larger sizes in parentheses.

NECKLACE

Setup

Using the dental floss threader, string beads onto yarn as follows (page 92):

25C, *[2A, 1B] 4 times, 12A; rep from * twice more, [2A, 1B] 4 times, 2A.

Using the knitted-on method (page 139), cast on 96 (104, 112) sts.

ROW 1: [K1, p1] 17 (19, 21) times, place marker, [k4, p2] 4 times, k4, place marker, [p1, k1] to end of row—28 sts between markers.

ROW 2: [P1, k1] to marker, [p4, k2] 4 times, p4, [k1, p1] to end of row.

ROW 3: [K1, p1] to marker, slip 1 bead, [k2tog, yo twice, ssk, slip 1 bead, p1, slip 1 bead, p1, slip 1 bead] 4 times, k2tog, yo twice, ssk, slip 1 bead, [p1, k1] to end of row.

ROW 4: [P1, k1] to marker, slip 1 bead, [p2, p1tbl, p1, slip 1 bead, k2, slip 1 bead] 4 times, p2, p1tbl, p1, slip 1 bead, [k1, p1] to end of row.

ROW 5: [K1, p1] to marker, slip 1 bead, [k2, yo twice, k2, slip 1 bead, p1, slip 1 bead, p1, slip 1 bead] 4 times, k2, yo twice, k2, slip 1 bead, [p1, k1] to end of row—38 sts between markers.

ROW 6: [P1, k1] to marker, slip 1 bead, [p3, p1tbl, p2, slip 1 bead, k2, slip 1 bead] 4 times, p3, p1tbl, p2, slip 1 bead, [k1, p1] to end of row.

ROW 7: [K1, p1] to marker, slip 1 bead, [k1, yo twice, k2, yo, k2, yo twice, k1, slip 1 bead, p1, slip 1 bead, p1, slip 1 bead] 4 times, k1, yo twice, k2, yo, k2, yo twice, k1, slip 1 bead, [p1, k1] to end of row—63 sts between markers.

ROW 8: [P1, k1] to marker, slip 1 bead, [p2, p1tbl, p6, p1tbl, p1, slip 1 bead, k2, slip 1 bead] 4 times, p2, p1tbl, p6, p1tbl, p1, slip 1 bead, [k1, p1] to end of row.

ROW 9: [K1, p1] to marker, slip 1 bead, [k3, yo twice, k2, yo, k1, yo, k2, yo twice, k3, slip 1 bead, p1,

slip 1 bead, p1, slip 1 bead] 4 times, k3, yo twice, k2, yo, k1, yo, k2, yo twice, k3, slip 1 bead, [p1, k1] to end of row—93 sts between markers.

BIND-OFF WITH BEADS

▶ **NOTE**: Work the bind-off loosely so the beads easily slip through the decreases. It helps to use a larger needle. Beads will go to the back of the right-hand needle when working into a stitch with a bead on it so that it lies on the front of the work. When you reach the double yarn over, work each yarn over as its own stitch. Resist the urge to work the second yarn over in the set through the back loop. Work it as the first one to keep the bind-off loose.

Working purlwise, work lace bind-off without a bead (plain) for 34 (38, 42) sts, *[lace bind-off with a bead once, lace bind-off plain for 3 sts] four times, lace bind-off with a bead once, lace bind-off plain for 2 sts; rep from * four more times, lace bind-off without a bead to the end (pages 93 and 140).

Weave in ends. Wet–block (page 140) to shape using pins to open up the ruffles. Sew clasp to the wrong side of the necklace with sewing needle and coordinating thread.

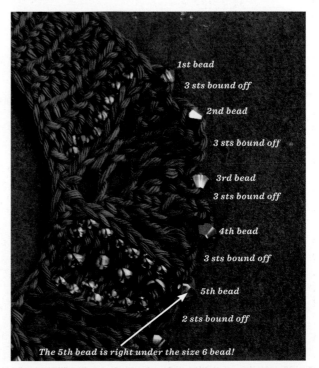

1st bead
3 sts bound off
2nd bead
3 sts bound off
3rd bead
3 sts bound off
4th bead
3 sts bound off
5th bead
2 sts bound off
The 5th bead is right under the size 6 bead!

This bottom-up tam plays with a modified beaded Coin Stitch ribbing. The Crown shaping incorporates the pattern so that it flows seamlessly to the bind-off. I did design matching mitts (page 107), but start with the tam since it's knit on larger needles and has minimal shaping.

» One of my knitting group buddies made a lovely cream-colored scarf using the Coin Stitch (a simple faux cable pattern) alternated with ribbing. Of course, my first thought was this: "Where are the beads?" So I ran home and fiddled with beads until I found out how to place the bead right at the base of the slipped stitch. Fun times!

CHA-CHING TAM

Skill level
Intermediate

Materials
- 160 yd (146m) light fingering-weight yarn (1)
- 168 size 6 glass seed beads (approximately 16 grams)
- US size 3 (3.25mm) 16" (40cm) circular needle, or size needed to obtain gauge
- US size 4 (3.5mm) 16" (40cm) circular needle, or size needed to obtain gauge
- US size 4 (3.5mm) double-pointed needles (or 1 long circular needle), or size needed to obtain gauge
- Dental floss threader
- Tapestry needle

Yarn Used
Manos del Uruguay *Fino;* 70% merino wool, 30% silk; 3½ oz (100g), 490 yd (448m); 1 skein in PocketWatch

Beads Used
6/0 Matsuno seed bead, transparent topaz with a silver-lined square hole and AB finish

Gauge
22 stitches and 34 rows = 4" (10cm) in stockinette stitch on larger needles, blocked
20 stitches and 32 rounds = 4" (10cm) in pattern on larger needles, blocked

Size
To fit an average adult head

Finished Measurements
Approximately 21" (53.5cm) around, stretched, x 8" (20.5cm) deep

Notes
- The Cha-Ching Stitch is both charted and written out. If you're working from the chart, remember to read every round from right to left, as the tam is worked in the round.

- The bead is placed on Round 3 of the pattern. Make sure the bead is on the right leg of the stitch so it lies in front of the work when you are working into that stitch on Round 4.

Special Stitch
CC3
Pass the third st on the left-hand needle over the first and second st on the left-hand needle, k1, yo, k1.

BRIM

Setup

Using a dental floss threader, string 168 beads onto the yarn (page 92).

With smaller circular needle, and using the long-tail method (page 138), cast on 108 sts, place marker, and join for working in the round, being careful not to twist the sts.

RIBBING ROUND: *K2, p2, k2, p3; rep from * to end of round.

Work the Ribbing Round as established 8 more times.

Switch to the larger circular needle and begin to work the Tam Body as follows:

INCREASE ROUND: *K1, m1R, k1f&b, p2, k1, m1R, k1, p3; rep from * around—144 sts.

TAM BODY

NOTE: If desired, place markers between repeats to help keep track of the pattern.

Work Rounds 1–4 of the Cha-Ching Stitch from the chart or the written instructions 10 times; you will be working the 12-stitch repeat twelve times each round.

CROWN DECREASES

NOTE: When sts start to stretch on the needle, switch to double-pointed needles or the Magic Loop technique (page 137).

Work Rounds 1–21 of the Crown Decreases from the chart or the written instructions once; you will be working the repeat 12 times each round—12 sts remain.

NEXT ROUND: K2tog around—6 sts remain.

Cut yarn leaving an 8" (20.5cm) tail, thread through remaining live sts to close up the top.

Weave in all ends and block. If desired, accentuate the shape by blocking (page 140) the tam over an 8" (20.5cm) plate.

CHA-CHING STITCH WRITTEN INSTRUCTIONS

(12-st repeat)

ROUND 1: K9, p3.

ROUND 2: CC3, k3, CC3, p3.

ROUND 3: K5, k1 with bead, k3, p3.

ROUND 4: K3, CC3, k3, p3.

CHA-CHING STITCH CROWN DECREASES WRITTEN INSTRUCTIONS

ROUND 1: K9, p3—12 sts per repeat.

ROUND 2: CC3, k3, CC3, p2tog, p1—(1 st decreased per repeat) 11 sts per repeat.

ROUND 3: K5, k1 with bead, k3, p2.

ROUND 4: K3, CC3, k1, k2tog, p2—10 sts per repeat.

ROUND 5: K8, p2.

ROUND 6: Pass the third st on the left-hand needle over the first and second sts on the left-hand needle, k4, CC3, p2—9 sts per repeat.

ROUND 7: K4, k1 with bead, k2, p2.

ROUND 8: K2, CC3, k2tog, p2—8 sts per repeat.

ROUND 9: K6, p2.

ROUND 10: Pass the third sts on the left-hand needle over the first and second sts on the left-hand needle, k2, CC3, p2—7 sts per repeat.

ROUND 11: K4, k1 with bead, p2.

ROUND 12: K2tog, CC3, p2—6 sts per repeat.

ROUND 13: K4, p2.

ROUND 14: CC3, k1, p2tog—5 sts per repeat.

ROUND 15: K3, k1 with bead, p1.

ROUND 16: K1, pass the third st on the left-hand needle over the first and second sts on the left-hand needle, k2, p1—4 sts per repeat.

ROUND 17: K3, p1.

ROUND 18: K1, k2tog, p1—3 sts per repeat.

ROUND 19: K2, p1.

ROUND 20: K2tog, p1—2 sts per repeat.

ROUND 21: K2tog—1 st per repeat.

CHA-CHING STITCH CHART (12-st repeat)

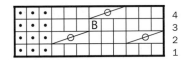

CHA-CHING STITCH CROWN DECREASES CHART

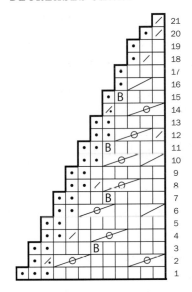

CHART KEY

☐ k1

• p1

B k1 with bead

⊘ CC3: pass the third st on your left-hand needle over the first and second stitches on the left-hand needle, then k1, yo, k1

⟋ pass the third st on your left-hand needle over the first and second stitches on the left-hand needle, then k2

⟋ p2tog

⟋ k2tog

How about some fitted fingerless mitts with a reverse stockinette stitch thumb gusset, and modified beaded Coin Stitch ribbing? Choose a durable yarn that can withstand the extra friction of the beads; keep this in mind if you choose to make the Cha-Ching Tam (page 103) in the same yarn.

» Your head and hands just have to match sometimes, don't you think? I loved the stitch I developed for the Cha-Ching Tam so much I had to design mitts with it as well. I also wanted to work with size 8 delica beads, a tubular-shaped bead that shows up perfectly on the stitch.

CHA-CHING MITTS

Skill level
Intermediate

Materials
- 200 (250) yd (183 [230]m) light fingering-weight yarn 🔟
- 120 (140) size 8 glass seed beads (approximately 5 [6] grams)
- US size 1.5 (2.5mm) double-pointed needles (or 1 long circular needle), or size needed to obtain gauge
- US size 1 (2.25mm) double-pointed needles (or 1 long circular needle), or size needed to obtain gauge
- Dental floss threader
- Stitch markers
- Scrap yarn (for stitch holder)
- Tapestry needle

Yarn Used
Stonehedge Fiber Mill *Shepherd's Wool Fingering;* 100% merino wool; 1.6 oz

(45g), 230 yd (210m); 1 (2) skeins in Raspberry

Beads Used
8/0 Miyuki delica seed bead, matte transparent mauve AB, color 0869

Gauge
32 stitches and 40 rows = 4" (10cm) in stockinette stitch on larger needles, blocked
36 stitches and 44 rounds = 4" (10cm) in pattern on larger needles, blocked

Size
Women's Small (Large)
Shown in Small
The pattern is written for multiple sizes. Instructions are given for size small, with larger size in parentheses.

Finished Measurements
To fit 7½ (8¼)" (19 [21]cm) hand circumference

Notes
- The Cha-Ching Stitch is charted and written out for both sizes. If you're working from the chart, remember to read every round from right to left as the mitts are worked in the round.

- The bead is placed on Round 3 of the pattern. Make sure the bead is on the right leg of the stitch so it lies in front of the work when you are working into that stitch on Round 4.

Special Stitch
CC3
Pass the third st on the left-hand needle over the first and second sts on the left-hand needle, k1, yo, k1.

MITTS

Setup

Using dental floss threader, string 60 (70) beads onto the yarn (page 92).

With smaller needles and using the long-tail method (page 138), cast on 53 (60) sts, and join for working in the round distributing sts on needles as preferred, being careful not to twist the sts. If desired, mark the beginning of the round with a removable stitch marker or safety pin.

RIBBING ROUND

For Small

*K3, p3, k3, p2, k3, p2; rep from * to last 5 sts, k3, p2.

For Large

*K3, p3; rep from * around.

Work Ribbing Round as established 6 more times.

Switch to larger needles and work Rounds 1–4 of the Cha-Ching Stitch from the chart or the written instructions for the size you are making 12 (14) times. You will be repeating the 16 (18) stitch repeat three times around.

NOTE: If desired, place markers between repeats to help keep track of the pattern.

SHAPE THUMB GUSSET

Continuing in pattern as established, work 46 (51) sts, place marker, p1f&b, p0 (1), p1f&b, place marker, work to end of round in pattern—2 sts increased.

Work 3 rounds as established in pattern, purling sts between gusset markers.

FOR RIGHT MITT: Discontinue using beads on the *first* column of beads.

FOR LEFT MITT: Discontinue using beads on the *last* column of beads.

This is so that the palm of the hand does not have beads, which would be uncomfortable!

ROUND 1: Work as established to marker, sl marker, p1f&b, p to 1 st before next marker, p1f&b, sl marker, work in pattern to end of round.

ROUNDS 2, 3, AND 4: Work around in pattern as established.

Repeat these 4 rounds 5 (6) times more, then work Rounds 1 and 2 once more—18 (21) thumb gusset sts.

NEXT ROUND: Work to marker in pattern, remove marker, slip 18 (21) thumb gusset sts onto length of scrap yarn, remove marker, using the backwards loop method (page 139), cast on 2 (3) sts over gap left by gusset, and work to end of round.

TOP

Continue working in pattern until 24 (28) pattern repeats have been worked from the beginning of the mitt, or to desired length, then work Rounds 1 and 2 once more.

Switch to smaller needles.

RIBBING ROUND

For Small

*K3, p3, (k3, p2) twice, rep from * to last 5 sts, k3, p2.

For Large

*K3, p3; rep from * to end of round.

Work ribbing round as established 3 more times.

Bind off in pattern, cut yarn leaving a 6" (15cm) tail, and pull through last st.

THUMB

With larger needles, return 18 (21) held thumb gusset sts to 3 needles. With right side facing, rejoin yarn and p18 (21), pick up and p4 tbl over gap and join for working in the round—22 (25) sts.

NEXT ROUND: P18 (21), p2tog twice—20 (23) sts remain.

Purl 5 (7) rounds or until thumb is desired length.

Knit 1 round.

Bind off, cut yarn leaving a 6" (15cm) tail, and pull through the last st.

Weave in ends and block (page 140).

CHA-CHING STITCH WRITTEN INSTRUCTIONS

For Small

ROUND 1: [K9, p2, k3, p2] 3 times, k3, p2.

ROUND 2: [CC3, k3, CC3, p2, k3, p2] 3 times, k3, p2.

ROUND 3: [K5, k1 with bead, (k3, p2) twice] 3 times, k3, p2.

ROUND 4: [K3, CC3, k3, p2, CC3, p2] 3 times, CC3, p2.

CHA-CHING STITCH WRITTEN INSTRUCTIONS

For Large

ROUND 1: [K9, p3, k3, p3] 3 times, k3, p3.

ROUND 2: [CC3, k3, CC3, p3, k3, p3] 3 times, k3, p3.

ROUND 3: [K5, k1 with bead, (k3, p3) twice] 3 times, k3, p3.

ROUND 4: [K3, CC3, k3, p3, CC3, p3] 3 times, CC3, p3.

*CHA-CHING STITCH CHART
SIZE SMALL*

End with
5 sts

Repeat blue box 3 times
(16-stitch repeat)

*CHA-CHING STITCH CHART
SIZE LARGE*

End with
6 sts

Repeat blue box 3 times
(18-stitch repeat)

CHART KEY

☐ k1

• p1

B k1 with bead

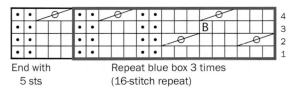 CC3: pass the 3rd st on your left-hand needle over the first and second stitches on the left-hand needle, then k1, yo, k1

Starting with a garter tab this semicircular, top-down, garter stitch–based shawl will get you comfortable with laceweight yarn and a variety of techniques. You've worked with the wrapped stitches skills learned in the first chapter, yarn overs from the second chapter, and finally, it's time to add the beads!

≫ This shawl is a perfect marriage of gradient yarn, elongated stitches, and beads. I designed my first semicircular shawl for my lace class with Craftsy.com, and have become enamored of its shaping ever since. Each section flows into the next so you never get bored with the knitting as it's constantly changing. All knitting should be like this! I adore the bottom edge with beads slipped up between the stitches on the wave stitch! What is your favorite part?

HALLI SHAWL

Skill level
Advanced Beginner

Materials
- 645 yd (586m) laceweight yarn 🔘①
- 324 size 8 round glass seed beads (approximately 10 grams)
- 1,054 size 8 triangular glass seed beads (approximately 40 grams)
- US size 5 (3.75mm) 24" (60cm) circular needle, or size needed to obtain gauge
- US size 5 (3.75mm) 40" (100cm) circular needle, or size needed to obtain gauge
- Dental floss threader
- Stitch markers
- Tapestry needle

Yarn Used
1 skein Knitwhits Freia Handpaints *Freia Ombré Lace;* 75% wool, 25% nylon; 2.65 oz (75g), 645 yd (590m); 1 skein in Denim

Beads Used
8/0 Miyuki round seed bead, transparent crystal with a silver-lining, color 131S
8/0 Toho triangular bead, transparent crystal and AB finish

Gauge
23 stitches and 38 rows = 4" (10cm) in stockinette stitch, blocked
23 stitches and 42 rows = 4" (10cm) in garter stitch, blocked

Finished Measurements
44" (112cm) across top x 22" (56cm) deep

Special Stitch
Wrap Stitch
*Slip 3 stitches purlwise with yarn in back onto the right-hand needle, bring yarn to front, slip stitches back to the left-hand needle, bring yarn to back; rep from * 3 times more, knit these 3 wrapped stitches.

SHAWL

Garter Tab
With shorter needle, and using the method of your choice, cast on 3 sts.

Knit 6 rows.

Turn work 90° clockwise, pick up and knit 3 sts along edge (1 in each garter ridge). Turn work 90° clockwise again, and pick up and knit 3 sts across cast-on edge—9 sts.

Section 1 (4 rows)
ROW 1 (INCREASE ROW): *K1, yo; rep from * to last st, k1—17 sts.

ROWS 2-4: Knit to end of row.

Section 2 (8 rows)
ROW 1 (INCREASE ROW): *K1, yo; rep from * to last st, k1f&b—34 sts.

ROWS 2-4: Knit to end of row.

ROW 5: Knit to end of row, wrapping yarn twice for each st.

ROW 6: Knit to end of row, dropping wraps as you come to them.

ROW 7-8: Knit to end of row.

Section 3 (10 rows)
ROW 1 (INCREASE ROW): *K1, yo; rep from * to the last st, k1—67 sts.

ROWS 2-4: Knit to end of row.

ROW 5: K2, *k1, k1 wrapping yarn twice, [k1 wrapping yarn 3 times] 3 times, k1 wrapping yarn twice, k2; rep from * across to last st, k1.

ROW 6: Knit to end of row, dropping wraps as you come to them.

ROW 7: K6, *k1, k1 wrapping yarn twice, [k1 wrapping yarn 3 times] 3 times, k1 wrapping yarn twice, k2; rep from * across to last 5 sts, k5.

ROW 8: Knit to end of row, dropping wraps as you come to them.

ROWS 9 AND 10: Knit to end of row.

Section 4 (24 rows)
ROW 1 (INCREASE ROW): *K1, yo; rep from * to the last 2 stitches, k2—132 sts.

ROWS 2 AND 3: Knit to end of row.

ROW 4: *[K1 wrapping yarn twice] twice, [k1 wrapping yarn 3 times] 3 times; rep from * to last 2 sts, [k1 wrapping yarn twice] twice.

ROW 5: K2 dropping extra wrap, *Wrap Stitch (over 3 sts), k2 dropping extra wrap; rep from * to end of row.

ROWS 6-9: Knit to end of row.

ROW 10: K2, *k1, k1 wrapping yarn twice, [k1 wrapping yarn 3 times] 3 times, k1 wrapping yarn twice, k2; rep from * to last 2 sts, k2.

ROW 11: Knit to end of row, dropping wraps as you come to them.

ROWS 12-15: Knit to end of row.

ROWS 16 AND 17: Repeat Rows 4 and 5.

ROWS 18-20: Knit to end of row.

ROW 21: Knit to end of row, wrapping yarn twice for each st.

ROW 22: Knit to end of row, dropping wraps as you come to them.

ROWS 23 AND 24: Knit to end of row.

Section 5 (34 rows)
NOTE: When sts become crowded on your needle, switch to the longer needle.

ROW 1 (INCREASE ROW): *K1, yo; rep from * to last st, k1f&b—264 sts.

ROWS 2-4: Knit to end of row.

ROW 5: Knit to end of row, wrapping yarn twice for each st.

ROW 6: Knit to end of row, dropping wraps as you come to them.

ROWS 7 AND 8: Knit to end of row.

Cut yarn leaving a 6" (15cm) tail and string on all 324 round beads, reattach yarn, and continue on with pattern (page 92).

ROW 9: [K1 wrapping yarn twice] twice, [k1 wrapping yarn twice with two beads] twice,*[k1 wrapping yarn twice] 8 times, [k1 wrapping yarn twice with 2 beads] twice; rep from * to end.

ROW 10: Beads should be to the *back of the left-hand needle* as you work this row: *Knit Criss-Cross 4, Knit Criss-Cross 6; rep from * 25 times more, Knit Criss-Cross 4.

ROW 11: Knit to end of row.

ROW 12: Knit to end of row, wrapping yarn 3 times for each st.

ROW 13: *Knit Criss-Cross 4, Knit Criss-Cross 6; rep from * 25 times more, Knit Criss-Cross 4.

ROW 14: Knit to end of row.

ROWS 15-17: Repeat Rows 12–14.

ROW 18: Repeat Row 9.

ROW 19: Beads should be to the *front of the left-hand needle* as you work this row: *Knit Criss-Cross 4, Knit Criss-Cross 6; rep from * 25 times more, Knit Criss-Cross 4.

ROW 20: Knit to end of row.

ROWS 21-26: Repeat Rows 12–17.

ROWS 27 AND 28: Repeat Rows 9–10.

ROW 29 AND 30: Knit to end of row.

ROWS 31-34: Repeat Rows 5–8.

Section 6 (22 rows)

ROW 1 (INCREASE ROW): *K1, yo; rep from * to last st, k1f&b—528 sts.

ROWS 2-4: Knit to end of row.

ROW 5: Knit to end of row, wrapping yarn twice for each st.

ROW 6: Knit to end of row, dropping wraps as you come to them.

ROW 7: Knit to end of row.

ROW 8: *K1, k1 wrapping yarn twice, [k1 wrapping yarn 3 times] 3 times, k1 wrapping yarn twice, k2; rep from * to end.

ROW 9: Knit to end of row, dropping wraps as you come to them.

ROWS 10-13: Knit to end of row.

ROW 14: K1 wrapping yarn twice, *[k1 wrapping yarn twice] twice, [k1 wrapping yarn 3 times] 3 times; rep from * to last 2 sts, [k1 wrapping yarn twice] twice.

ROW 15: K2 dropping extra wrap, *Wrap Stitch (over 3 sts), k2 dropping extra wrap; rep from * to last st, k1 dropping extra wrap.

ROWS 16 AND 17: Knit to end of row.

Cut yarn string on 527 triangular beads, reattach yarn and continue on with pattern.

ROW 18: *K1, slip 1 bead; rep from * to last st, k1.

ROW 19: *K1, k1 wrapping yarn twice, [k1 wrapping yarn 3 times] 3 times, k1 wrapping yarn twice, k2; rep from * to end of row.

Cut yarn and string on 527 triangular beads with dental floss threader (page 92).

ROW 20: *K1, slip 1 bead; rep from * across to last st, k1, dropping wraps as you reach them.

ROWS 21 AND 22: Knit to end of row.

Bind off. Weave in ends and block (page 140).

Laden is chock-full of texture and techniques to tickle your fancy. This faux Möbius cowl (or "fauxbius") starts with a provisional cast-on. Then a length of reversible cables and double-sided lace is knit with or without beads. Finally, the rectangle is twisted, grafted, and banded to hide the seam. What fun!

» The juxtaposition of reversible cables and double-sided lace makes me swoon! Heavy cables play against this delicate lace stitch, creating an unexpected fabric that flows around the neck and shoulders beautifully. Cowls are a much-loved accessory in my wardrobe. As soon as the first Laden was finished, I had to knit another version with beads! Once you see how I've added beads to a previously plain pattern, you may well be inspired to reimagine another pattern in this book with beads.

LADEN FAUXBIUS

Skill level
Advanced

Materials
- 610 (710) yd (558 [650]m) fingering-weight yarn (1)
- 2,916 (3,402) size 8 glass seed beads (85 [100] grams)
- US size 5 (3.75mm) needles or size needed to obtain gauge
- US size 4 (3.5mm) needles or one size smaller than needed to obtain gauge
- Cable needle or spare double-pointed needle
- Stitch holder or spare needle
- Scrap yarn
- Crochet hook (optional)
- Dental floss threader (optional)
- Tapestry needle

Yarn Used
Knitted Wit *Fingering;* 100% superwash merino wool; 3½ oz (100g), 400 yd (365m); 2 skeins in Cedar
Lorna's Laces *Solemate;* 55% superwash merino wool, 15% nylon, 30% Outlast viscose; 3½ oz (100g), 425 yd (389m); 2 skeins in Dobson

Bead Used (optional)
8/0 Miyuki seed bead, transparent olive with a silver lining and AB finish

Gauge
22 stitches and 30 rows = 4" (10cm) in stockinette stitch, blocked

Size
Women's Small (Large)
Gray shown in Small; green shown in Large
The pattern is written for multiple sizes. Instructions are given for size small, with larger size in parentheses.

Finished Measurements
10" (25.5cm) wide x 36 (42)" (91 [106.5]cm) around

Note
- The stitches for Laden are both charted and written out. If you're working from the chart, remember that the odd-numbered rows are read right to left and the even-numbered rows from left to right to work the cowl flat.

LADEN FAUXBIUS

OPTIONAL: Using the dental floss threader, string 486 size 8 beads onto the yarn (page 92).

NOTE: This is enough beads to work 3 repeats of the Lace Chart. When you finish the 3 repeats, cut the yarn and string on more, for a grand total of 2,916 (3,402) beads. Don't thread them all on at once (see "Prestrung Beads: Tips and Tricks," page 90).

NOTE: Ignore instructions for working with beads, if you choose to knit a beadless Laden.

PROVISIONAL CAST-ON: With scrap yarn using the crochet method (page 139), cast on 93 sts onto larger needle, then single crochet a few extra stitches. Cut yarn, leaving a 6" (15cm) tail, pull through last crochet stitch, and tie a knot.

SETUP ROW (WS): With working yarn, purl 1 row.

ROW 1: K1, [work Row 1 of Cable Stitch, work Row 1 of Lace Stitch] 3 times, work Row 1 of Cable Stitch once more, k1.

ROW 2: K1, [work Row 2 of Cable Stitch, work Row 2 of Lace Stitch] 3 times, work Row 2 of Cable Stitch once more, k1.

Continue as established, until 18 (21) repeats of the Lace Stitch and 6 (7) repeats of the Cable Stitch are complete.

Cut yarn leaving a 72" (183cm) tail for grafting the ends.

Thread live sts onto scrap yarn and wet-block (page 140) rectangle to approximately 10" (25.5cm) wide and 36 (42)" (91 [106.5]cm) long. Move sts from both the live end and the provisional cast-on end onto separate needles. Flip one end over so that there is a twist in the fabric. Holding needles parallel to each other, Kitchener stitch together (page 138). Weave in ends.

BAND *(worked without beads)*

PROVISIONAL CAST-ON: With scrap yarn using the crochet method (page 139), cast on 43 sts onto smaller needle, then single crochet a few extra stitches. Cut yarn, leaving a 6" (15cm) tail, pull through the last crochet stitch, and tie a knot.

SETUP ROW (WS): With working yarn, purl 1 row.

Ignoring instructions for working with beads, continue as follows:

ROW 1: K1, work Row 1 of Cable Stitch, work Row 1 of Lace Stitch, work Row 1 of Cable Stitch, k1.

ROW 2: K1, work Row 2 of Cable Stitch, work Row 2 of Lace Stitch, work Row 2 of Cable Stitch, k1.

LACE STITCH WITH BEADS CHART (9 STS)

CHART KEY

╱	k2tog (RS), p2tog (WS)
╲	p2tog (RS), k2tog (WS)
(light gray)	bead to back (see notes)
(dark gray)	bead to front (see notes)
②	yo with 2 beads
③	yo with 3 beads
④	yo with 4 beads
⑤	yo with 5 beads
□	k1 (RS), p1 (WS)
•	p1 (RS), k1 (WS)
O	yo

Ignore directions for beads and work yarn overs plain if you choose to knit a beadless Laden.

Continue as established, until 46 rows are complete (Rows 1–46 of the Cable Stitch, and Rows 1–16 twice and Rows 1–14 once more of the Lace Stitch). Cut yarn leaving a 36" (91cm) tail for grafting the ends.

FINISHING

Thread live sts onto scrap yarn and wet-block rectangle to approximately 3½" (9cm) wide by 6" (15cm) long. Move sts from both the live end and the provisional cast-on end onto separate needles. Place Band around join on the Mobius, hiding graft in the twist. Holding needles parallel to each other, and without twisting the band, use Kitchener stitch to graft the sts together. If desired, fasten band in place over the twist. Weave in ends.

CHART KEY

☐   k1 (RS), p1 (WS)

•   p1 (RS), k1 (WS)

slip 8 sts to cable needle, hold in front of work,
[k1, p1] four times, then work
[p1, k1] four times from cable needle

CABLE STITCH CHART (16 sts)

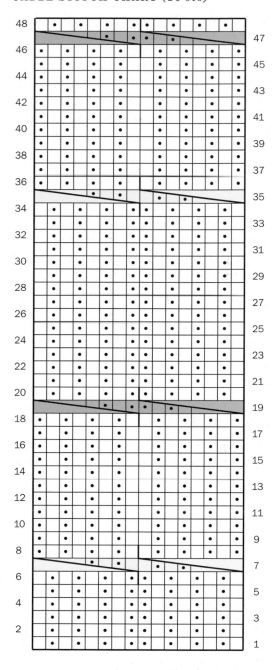

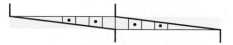

slip 8 sts to cable needle, hold in front of work,
[p1, k1] four times, then work
[k1, p1] four times from cable needle

LACE STITCH WRITTEN INSTRUCTIONS *(9 sts)*

NOTE: Underlined stitches have beads held to the back. *Italic* stitches have beads held to the front. Ignore these directions if you aren't working with beads, and work yarn overs plain.

ROW 1: K2, k2tog, k3, <u>k1</u>, yo with 3 beads, p1.

ROW 2: <u>K1</u>, yo with 2 beads, *p1*, p3, p2tog, p2.

ROW 3: K2tog, yo, k2tog, k3, yo with 3 beads, *p1*, p1.

ROW 4: K2, <u>k1</u>, yo with 3 beads, p2, p2tog, p2.

ROW 5: K2tog, yo, k2tog, k1, yo with 4 beads, *p1*, p3.

ROW 6: K4, <u>k1</u>, yo with 5 beads, p2tog, p2.

ROW 7: K1, k2tog, yo with 4 beads, *p1*, p5.

ROW 8: K6, <u>k1</u>, yo with 3 beads, p2tog.

ROW 9: K1, yo with 3 beads, *p1*, p3, p2tog, p2.

ROW 10: K2, k2tog, k3, <u>k1</u>, yo with 2 beads, p1.

ROW 11: K1, <u>k1</u>, yo with 3 beads, p3, p2tog, yo, p2tog.

ROW 12: K2, k2tog, k2, yo with 3 beads, *p1*, p2.

ROW 13: K3, <u>k1</u>, yo with 4 beads, p1, p2tog, yo, p2tog.

ROW 14: K2, k2tog, yo with 5 beads, *p1*, p4.

ROW 15: K5, <u>k1</u>, yo with 4 beads, p2tog, p1.

ROW 16: K2tog, yo with 3 beads, *p1*, p6.

CABLE STITCH WRITTEN INSTRUCTIONS *(16 sts)*

ROWS 1, 3, AND 5 (RS): [K1, p1] 4 times, [p1, k1] 4 times.

ROWS 2, 4, AND 6 (WS): [P1, k1] 4 times, [k1, p1] 4 times.

ROW 7: Slip 8 sts onto cable needle, hold in front of work, [p1, k1] 4 times, then work [k1, p1] 4 times from cable needle.

ROWS 8, 10, 12, 14, 16, AND 18: [K1, p1] 4 times, [p1, k1] 4 times.

ROWS 9, 11, 13, 15, AND 17: [P1, k1] 4 times, [k1, p1] 4 times.

ROW 19: Slip 8 sts onto cable needle, hold in front of work, [k1, p1] 4 times, then work [p1, k1] 4 times from cable needle.

ROWS 20, 22, 24, 26, 28, 30, 32, AND 34: Repeat Row 2.

ROWS 21, 23, 25, 27, 29, 31, AND 33: Repeat Row 1.

ROW 35: Repeat Row 7.

ROWS 36, 38, 40, 42, 44, AND 46: Repeat Row 8.

ROWS 37, 39, 41, 43, AND 45: Repeat Row 9.

ROW 47: Repeat Row 19.

ROW 48: Repeat Row 2.

This scarf is knit from the center down one side, then stitches are picked up and the second half is worked the same as the first. You'll begin with a diagonal Eyelet Stitch that incorporates beads as you reach the last quarter of the scarf. Finally a gentle beaded lace ruffle is worked at the bottom edge.

≫ When I was finishing my Trapeze Shawl Mystery Knit-Along, one of the participating knitters asked if I could design a scarf that used the same bicolored beaded ruffle. When I first conceptualized the scarf, the beading was worked throughout, but I quickly realized it would become too heavy. By gradually incorporating the beads, I was still able to utilize the beaded Eyelet Stitch as a design detail without adding excess weight.

TRAPEZE SCARF

Skill level
Advanced

Materials
- 470 yd (430m) light fingering-weight yarn (1)
- 864 size 8 glass seed beads (approximately 25 grams) (color A)
- 264 size 8 glass seed beads (approximately 10 grams) (color C)
- US size 4 (3.5mm) needles, or size needed to obtain gauge
- Smooth scrap yarn
- Size E-4 (3.5mm) crochet hook
- Dental floss threader
- Tapestry needle

Yarn Used
Fibre Company *Meadow;* 40% baby merino wool, 25% baby llama, 20% mulberry silk, 15% linen; 3½ oz (100g), 549 yd (502m); 1 skein in Prairie

Beads Used
8/0 Matsuno seed bead, transparent topaz with AB gold wash, color 257 (color A)
8/0 Toho seed bead, transparent raspberry with silver-lined square hole, color 2226 (color C)

Gauge
22 stitches and 28 rows = 4" (10cm) in stockinette stitch, blocked
18 stitches and 27 rows = 4" (10cm) in pattern stitch, blocked

Finished Measurements
10" (25.5cm) wide x 68" (172.5cm) long

Notes
- Choose beads that contrast well with each other *and* the yarn. I chose color A to coordinate with the yarn and color C to pop (or contrast) against both the yarn and bead A.

- The stitches for this pattern are both charted and written out. If you're working from the chart, remember that the odd-numbered rows are read from right to left and the even-numbered rows from left to right to work the scarf flat.

FIRST HALF

PROVISIONAL CAST-ON: With scrap yarn and using the crochet method (page 139), cast on 45 sts, then single crochet a few extra stitches. Cut yarn, leaving a 6" (15cm) tail, pull through last crochet stitch, and tie a knot.

SETUP ROW (WS): With working yarn, purl 1 row.

Work Rows 1–10 of the Eyelet Stitch from the chart (page 125) or the written instructions 16 times.

If you're reading the chart, work to the blue box, work the sts in the blue box 3 times, work the 11 center sts, work the sts in the blue box 3 times, then complete the row as charted.

Cut the yarn and string on 360 A beads (page 92).

Work Rows 1–70 of the Beaded Eyelet Stitch (page 128) from the chart or the written instructions once.

BOTTOM BORDER AND BIND-OFF

Cut yarn leaving a 6" (15cm) tail and string on beads as follows: 50C [11C (2A, 2C, 2A, 1C) three times] twice, 10C [(1C, 4A) three times, 5C] four times (page 92).

Work Rows 1–13 of the Trapeze Bottom Border Stitch from the chart (page 127) or the written instructions once. If you're reading the chart, work to the blue box, repeat sts in the blue box 3 times, then complete the row as charted.

LACE BIND-OFF WITH BEADS

NOTE: Work the bind-off loosely so the beads will easily slip through the decreases. Beads will go to the back of the left-hand needle when working into a stitch with a bead on it so that it lies on the front of the work (page 93).

Setup
P2, insert the left-hand needle into the back of the 2 sts on the right-hand needle, purl them together

with 1 bead. P1 (you will have 2 stitches on the right-hand needle), insert the left-hand needle into the back of the 2 sts on the right-hand needle, purl them together.

Then P1, insert the left-hand needle into the back of the 2 sts on the right-hand needle, purl together with 1 bead.

P1, insert the left-hand needle into the back of the 2 sts on the right-hand needle, purl them together.

Repeat 2-st bind-off pattern until all sts are bound off. Cut yarn and pull through last st.

SECOND HALF

Remove scrap yarn from the provisional cast-on and return sts to a needle—45 sts.

NOTE: This is easier to do with a needle smaller than the working needle; transfer to the working needle once you have "caught" all the sts. Also, do not be surprised if you find that you have 1 more or 1 less stitch on the next row. It's tricksy to pick up the stitches and line up the lace pattern. You may have a "make it work" moment here!

With wrong side facing, reattach yarn.

K2, purl to last 2 sts, k2.

Work as for the first half of the scarf beginning with: Work Rows 1–10 of the Eyelet Stitch.

Weave in all ends and block (page 140) to measurements.

EYELET STITCH WRITTEN INSTRUCTIONS

ROW 1 (RS): K2, [k3, k2tog, yo] 3 times, k3, k2tog, yo, k1, yo, ssk, k3, [yo, ssk, k3] 3 times, k2.

ROWS 2, 4, 6, 8, AND 10 (WS): K2, purl to last 2 sts, k2.

ROW 3: K2, [k2, k2tog, yo, k1] 3 times, k2, k2tog, yo, k3, yo, ssk, k2, [k1, yo, ssk, k2] 3 times, k2.

ROW 5: K2, [k1, k2tog, yo, k2] 3 times, k1, k2tog, yo, k5, yo, ssk, k1, [k2, yo, ssk, k1] 3 times, k2.

ROW 7: K2, [k2tog, yo, k3] 3 times, k2tog, yo, k7, yo, ssk, [k3, yo, ssk] 3 times, k2.

ROW 9: K1, k2tog, [yo, k3, k2tog] 3 times, yo, k9, yo, [ssk, k3, yo] 3 times, ssk, k1.

BEADED EYELET STITCH WRITTEN INSTRUCTIONS

NOTE: Underlined stitches have beads held to the back. *Italic* stitches have beads held to the front.

ROW 1 (RS): K2, [k3, k2tog, yo] 4 times, k1, [yo, ssk, k3] 4 times, k2.

ROWS 2, 4, AND 6 (WS): K2, purl to last 2 sts, k2.

ROW 3: K2, [k2, k2tog, yo, k1] 4 times, k1, [k1, yo, ssk, k2] 4 times, k2.

ROW 5: K2, [k1, k2tog, yo, k2] 4 times, k1, [k2, yo, ssk, k1] 4 times, k2.

ROW 7: K2, [k2tog, yo, k3] 4 times, k1, [k3, yo, ssk] 4 times, k2.

ROW 8: K2, p19, [p1 with bead, p1] twice, purl to last 2 sts, k2.

ROW 9: K1, [k2tog, yo, k3] 4 times, k1, k1, *k1*, [k3, yo, ssk] 4 times, k1.

ROW 10: Repeat Row 8.

ROW 11: K2, [k3, k2tog, yo] 3 times, k3, k2tog, yo, k1, yo, *ssk*, k3, [yo, ssk, k3] 3 times, k2.

ROW 12: K2, p18, [p1 with bead] twice, p1, [p1 with bead] twice, purl to last 2 sts, k2.

ROW 13: K2, [k2, k2tog, yo, k1] 3 times, k2, k2tog, yo, *k1*, k1, k1, yo, *ssk*, k2, [k1, yo, ssk, k2] 3 times, k2.

ROW 14: K2, p17, [p1 with bead] twice, p3, [p1 with bead] twice, purl to last 2 sts, k2.

ROW 15: K1, [k2, k2tog, yo, k1] 3 times, k2, k2tog, yo, *k1*, k3, k1, yo, *ssk*, k2, [k1, yo, ssk, k2] 3 times, k1.

ROW 16: K2, p16, [p1 with bead] twice, p5, [p1 with bead] twice, purl to the last 2 sts, k2.

ROW 17: K2, [k2tog, yo, k3] 3 times, k2tog, yo, *k1*, k5, k1, yo, *ssk*, [k3, yo, ssk] 3 times, k2.

ROW 18: K2, p15, [p1 with bead] twice, p2, p1 with bead, p1, p1 with bead, p2, [p1 with bead] twice, purl to last 2 sts, k2.

ROW 19: K1, [k2tog, yo, k3] 3 times, k2tog, yo, *k1*, k2, k1, k1, *k1*, k2, k1, yo, *ssk*, [k3, yo, ssk] 3 times, k1.

ROW 20: K2, p14, [p1 with bead] twice, p3, p1 with bead, p1, p1 with bead, p3, [p1 with bead] twice, purl to last 2 sts, k2.

ROW 21: K2, [k3, k2tog, yo] twice, k3, k2tog, yo, *k1*, k2, k2tog, yo, k1, yo, *ssk*, k2, k1, yo, *ssk*, [k3, yo, ssk] twice, k5.

ROW 22: K2, p13, [p1 with bead] twice, p3, [p1 with bead] twice, p1, [p1 with bead] twice, p3, [p1 with bead] twice, purl to last 2 sts, k2.

ROW 23: K2, [k2, k2tog, yo, k1] twice, [k2, k2tog, yo, *k1*] twice, k1, [k1, yo, *ssk*, k2] twice, [k1, yo, ssk, k2] twice, k2.

ROW 24: K2, p12, [(p1 with bead) twice, p3] four times, purl to last 2 sts, k2.

ROW 25: K3, [k2tog, yo, k3] twice, [k2tog, yo, *k1,* k2] twice, k1, [k1, yo, *ssk,* k2] twice, k1, [yo, ssk, k3] twice.

ROW 26: K2, p11, [p1 with bead] twice, p3, [p1 with bead] twice, p5, [p1 with bead] twice, p3, [p1 with bead] twice, purl to last 2 sts, k2.

ROW 27: K2, [k2tog, yo, k3] twice, [k2tog, yo, *k1,* k2] twice, k1, [k2, k1, yo, *ssk*] twice, [k3, yo, ssk] twice, k2.

ROW 28: K2, p10, [p1 with bead] twice, p3, [p1 with bead] twice, p2, p1 with bead, p1, p1 with bead, p2, [p1 with bead] twice, p3, [p1 with bead] twice, purl to last 2 sts, k2.

ROW 29: K1, [k2tog, yo, k3] twice, [k2tog, yo, *k1,* k2] twice, k1, k1, *k1,* [k2, k1, yo, *ssk*] twice, [k3, yo, ssk] twice, k1.

ROW 30: K2, p9, [(p1 with bead) twice, p3] twice, p1 with bead, p1, p1 with bead, [p3, (p1 with bead) twice] twice, purl to last 2 sts, k2.

ROW 31: K5, k2tog, yo, k1, [k2, k2tog, yo, *k1*] twice, k2, k2tog, yo, k1, yo, *ssk,* k2, [k1, yo, *ssk,* k2] twice, k1, yo, ssk, knit to end.

ROW 32: K2, p8, [(p1 with bead) twice, p3] twice, [p1 with bead] twice, p1, [p1 with bead] twice, (p3, [p1 with bead] twice) twice, purl to last 2 sts, k2.

ROW 33: K4, k2tog, yo, k1, [k2, k2tog, yo, *k1*] 3 times, k1, [k1, yo, *ssk,* k2] 3 times, k1, yo, ssk, knit to end.

ROW 34: K2, p7, [(p1 with bead) twice, p3] 6 times, purl to last 2 sts, k2.

ROW 35: K3, k2tog, yo, k3, [k2tog, yo, *k1,* k2] 3 times, k1, [k1, yo, *ssk,* k2] 3 times, k1, yo, ssk, knit to end.

ROW 36: K2, p6, [(p1 with bead) twice, p3] 3 times, p2, [(p1 with bead) twice, p3] 3 times, purl to last 2 sts, k2.

ROW 37: K2, k2tog, yo, k3, [k2tog, yo, *k1,* k2] 3 times, k1, [k2, k1, yo, *ssk*] 3 times, k3, yo, ssk, knit to end.

ROW 38: K2, p5, [(p1 with bead) twice, p3] twice, [p1 with bead] twice, p2, p1 with bead, p1, p1 with bead, p2, [(p1 with bead) twice, p3] 3 times, p2, k2.

ROW 39: K1, k2tog, yo, k3, [k2tog, yo, *k1,* k2] 3 times, k1, k1, *k1,* [k2, k1, yo, *ssk*] 3 times, k3, yo, ssk, k1.

ROW 40: K2, p4, [(p1 with bead) twice, p3] 3 times, p1 with bead, p1, p1 with bead, [p3, (p1 with bead) twice] 3 times, purl to last 2 sts, k2.

ROW 41: K5, [k2tog, yo, *k1,* k2] 3 times, k2tog, yo, k1, yo, *ssk,* [k2, k1, yo, *ssk*] 3 times, k5.

EYELET STITCH CHART

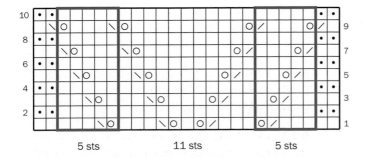

5 sts   11 sts   5 sts

Work blue box repeats three times each

CHART KEY

☐ k1 (RS), p1 (WS)

• p1 (RS), k1 (WS)

○ yo

╱ k2tog

╲ ssk

ROW 42: K2, [p3, (p1 with bead) twice] 4 times, p1, [(p1 with bead) twice, p3] 4 times, k2.

ROW 43: K2, [k2, k2tog, yo, *k1*] 4 times, k1, [k1, yo, *ssk,* k2] 4 times, k2.

ROW 44: K2, p2, [(p1 with bead) twice, p3] 7 times, [p1 with bead] twice, p2, k2.

ROW 45: K3, [k2tog, yo, *k1,* k2] 4 times, k1, [k1, yo, *ssk,* k2] 4 times, k1.

ROW 46: K2, p1, [(p1 with bead) twice, p3] 4 times, p2, [(p1 with bead) twice, p3] 3 times, [p1 with bead] twice, p1, k2.

ROW 47: [K2, k2tog, yo, *k1*] 4 times, k5, [k1, yo, *ssk,* k2] 4 times.

ROW 48: K2, [(p1 with bead) twice, p3] 3 times, [p1 with bead] twice, p2, p1 with bead, p1, p1 with bead, p2, [(p1 with bead) twice, p3] 3 times, [p1 with bead] twice, k2.

ROW 49: K1, [k2tog, yo, *k1,* k2] 4 times, k1, k1, *k1,* [k2, k1, yo, *ssk*] 4 times, k1.

ROW 50: K2, p4, [(p1 with bead) twice, p3] 3 times, p1 with bead, p1, p1 with bead, [p3, (p1 with bead) twice] 3 times, purl to last 2 sts, k2.

ROWS 51–60: Repeat Rows 41–50.

ROWS 61–67: Repeat Rows 41–47.

ROW 68: K2, [(p1 with bead) twice, p3] 4 times, p1, [p3, (p1 with bead) twice] 4 times, k2.

ROW 69: K1, [k2tog, yo, *k1,* k2] 4 times, k3, [k2, k1, yo, *ssk*] 4 times, k1.

ROW 70: K2, purl to the last 2 sts, k2.

TRAPEZE BOTTOM BORDER STITCH WRITTEN INSTRUCTIONS

NOTE: Underlined stitches have beads held to the back. *Italic* stitches have beads held to the front.

ROW 1 (RS): K2, yo, p1, slip bead, p1, yo, [k3, k2tog, yo, k1, yo, ssk, k3, yo, p1, slip bead, p1, yo] 3 times, k2—53 sts.

ROW 2 (WS): K2, [p1, k1, slip bead, k1, p4, (p1 with bead) twice, p1, (p1 with bead) twice, p3] 3 times, p1, k1, slip bead, k1, p1, k2.

ROW 3: K3, yo, p1, slip bead, p1, yo, [k3, k2tog, yo, *k1,* k1, k1, yo, *ssk,* k3, yo, p1, slip bead, p1, yo] 3 times, k3—61 sts.

ROW 4: K2, p1, [p1, k1, slip bead, k1, p4, (p1 with bead) twice, p3, (p1 with bead) twice, p3] 3 times, p1, k1, slip bead, k1, p2, k2.

ROW 5: K4, yo, p1, slip bead, p1, yo, [k3, k2tog, yo, *k1*, k3, k1, yo, *ssk*, k3, yo, p1, slip bead, p1, yo] 3 times, k4—69 sts.

ROW 6: K2, p2, [p1, k1, slip bead, k1, p4, (p1 with bead) twice, p5, (p1 with bead) twice, p3] 3 times, p1, k1, slip bead, k1, p3, k2.

ROW 7: K5, yo, p1, slip bead, p1, yo, [k3, k2tog, yo, *k1*, k5, k1, yo, *ssk*, k3, yo, p1, slip bead, p1, yo] 3 times, k5—77 sts.

ROW 8: K2, p3, [p1, k1, slip bead, k1, p4, (p1 with bead) twice, p7, (p1 with bead) twice, p3] 3 times, p1, k1, slip bead, k1, p4, k2.

ROW 9: K6, yo, p1, slip bead, p1, yo, [k3, k2tog, yo, *k1*, k2, p1, slip bead, p1, slip bead, p1, k2, k1, yo, *ssk*, k3, yo, p1, slip bead, p1, yo] 3 times, k6—85 sts.

ROW 10: K2, p4, [p1, k1, slip bead, k1, p4, (p1 with bead) twice, p3, k1, slip bead, k1, slip bead, k1, p3, (p1 with bead) twice, p3] 3 times, p1, k1, slip bead, k1, p5, k2.

ROW 11: K7, yo, p1, slip bead, p1, yo, [k3, k2tog, yo, *k1*, k3, p1, slip bead, p1, slip bead, p1, k3, k1, yo, *ssk*, k3, yo, p1, slip bead, p1, yo] 3 times, k7—93 sts.

ROW 12: K2, p5, [p1, k1, slip bead, k1, p4, (p1 with bead) twice, p4, k1, slip bead, k1, slip bead, k1, p4, (p1 with bead) twice, p3] 3 times, p1, k1, slip bead, k1, p6, k2.

ROW 13: K8, yo, p1, slip bead, p1, yo, [k3, k2tog, yo, *k1*, k4, p1, slip bead, p1, slip bead, p1, k4, k1, yo, *ssk*, k3, yo, p1, slip bead, p1, yo] 3 times, k8—101 sts.

TRAPEZE BOTTOM BORDER STITCH CHART

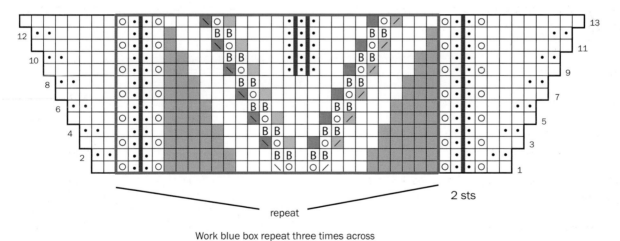

repeat

2 sts

Work blue box repeat three times across
Repeat begins with 13 sts

CHART KEY

☐ k1 (RS), p1 (WS)

• p1 (RS), k1 (WS)

○ yo

╱ k2tog

B p1 with bead

▨ bead to back (see notes)

▨ bead to front (see notes)

╲ ssk

❚❚ slip bead

▨ no stitch

BEADED EYELET STITCH CHART (45 sts)

NOTE: Chart is given full size, not broken down for repeats, since it is much easier to read this way. The repeats change row by row, making for a confusing-looking chart, and I chose to simplify it for you. Refer to the written instructions for repeat information.

This reversible double-sided lace scarf features beads that graduate in color inside each wave of the lace stitch. The beads are prestrung in a sequence so that they fall in the correct place. You can use just one color bead, if you desire, and it will still be gorgeous!

≫ Sometimes I look back on previous designs and suddenly see how to work them differently—not necessarily better, but maybe more resolved. In this case I turned to my first beaded design, Undulating Waves, and thought about how I could change the stitch to be reversible. Then (because who wants to be boring?), I threaded the beads to create color shifts in each wave.

REVERSIBLE UNDULATING WAVES SCARF

Skill level
Advanced

Materials
- 300 yd (275m) fingering-weight yarn
  (1)
- 648 size 6 glass seed beads (approximately 65 grams) (B, bigger)
- 540 size 8 glass seed beads (approximately 15 grams) (A, smaller)
- US size 5 (3.75mm) needles, or size needed to obtain gauge
- Dental floss threader
- Tapestry needle

Yarn Used
Koigu *KPPPM*; 100% superwash merino wool; 1¾ oz (50g), 175 yd (160m); color 285

Beads Used
6/0 Matsuno seed bead, transparent topaz with silver-lined square hole, and AB finish (B)
8/0 Toho seed bead, transparent aqua with gold lining (A)

Gauge
22 stitches and 28 rows = 4" (10cm) in stockinette stitch, blocked
20 stitches and 28 rows = 4" (10cm) in pattern stitch, blocked

Finished Measurements
6" (15cm) x 46" long (117cm)

Notes

- Choose beads that contrast with each other *and* the yarn color so that they don't get lost.

- The Undulating Waves Stitch is both charted and written out. If you're reading from the chart, remember that the odd-numbered rows are read from right to left and the even-numbered rows from left to right to work the scarf flat.

SETUP

Using the dental floss threader, string beads onto yarn as follows: [15A, 18B] 12 times (page 92).

Using the long-tail method (page 138), cast on 36 sts.

BORDER

ROWS 1 AND 2: Knit to last 3 sts, slip last 3 sts purlwise with yarn in front.

ROW 3: K1, k1 wrapping yarn twice, k to last 3 sts, slip the last 3 sts purlwise with yarn in front.

ROW 4: K1, k1 wrapping yarn twice, k to last 3 sts, slip last 3 sts purlwise with yarn in front, dropping the extra wrap when you reach it.

ROW 5: Knit to last 3 sts, slip last 3 sts purlwise with yarn in front, dropping the extra wrap when you reach it.

ROW 6: Repeat Row 1.

BEGIN UNDULATING WAVES STITCH

ROW 1: K1, k1 wrapping yarn twice, k1, [work Row 1 from chart or written instructions] 3 times, slip last 3 sts purlwise with yarn in front.

ROW 2: K1, k1 wrapping yarn twice, k1, [work Row 2 from chart or written instructions] 3 times, slip last 3 sts purlwise with yarn in front, dropping the extra wrap when you reach it.

ROW 3: K3, [work Row 3 from chart or written instructions] 3 times, slip last 3 sts purlwise with yarn in front, dropping the extra wrap when you reach it.

ROW 4: K3, [work Row 4 from chart or written instructions] 3 times, slip last 3 sts purlwise with yarn in front.

Continue edging as established working Rows 1–18 of the chart 18 times total.

NOTE: It can help to place a removable stitch marker on the right side of the work.

When the beads run out, cut yarn and thread on more as follows: [15A, 18B] 12 times.

When the beads run out again, cut yarn and thread once more as follows: [15A, 18B] 12 times.

Work Rows 1–5 of Border again.

Knit 1 row.

Bind off. Weave in ends and block (page 140).

REVERSIBLE UNDULATING WAVES WRITTEN INSTRUCTIONS *(10-st repeat)*

NOTE: Underlined stitches have beads held to the back. *Italic* stitches have beads held to the front.

ROW 1: Yo with 3 beads, k8, k2tog.

ROW 2: P2tog, p7, yo with 2 beads, *k1.*

ROW 3: P1, p1, yo with bead, k6, k2tog.

ROW 4: P2tog, p5, yo with bead, *k1,* k2.

ROW 5: P3, p1, yo with bead, k4, k2tog.

ROW 6: P2tog, p3, yo with bead, *k1,* k4.

ROW 7: P5, p1, yo with bead, k2, k2tog.

ROW 8: P2tog, p1, yo with bead, *k1,* k6.

ROW 9: P7, p1, yo, k2tog.

ROW 10: Yo with 3 beads, k8, k2tog.

ROW 11: P2tog, p7, yo with 2 beads, *k1.*

ROW 12: P1, p1, yo with bead, k6, k2tog.

ROW 13: P2tog, p5, yo with bead, *k1,* k2.

ROW 14: P3, p1, yo with bead, k4, k2tog.

ROW 15: P2tog, p3, yo with bead, *k1,* k4.

ROW 16: P5, p1, yo with bead, k2, k2tog.

ROW 17: P2tog, p1, yo with bead, *k1,* k6.

ROW 18: P7, p1, yo, k2tog.

REVERSIBLE UNDULATING WAVES CHART *(10-st repeat)*

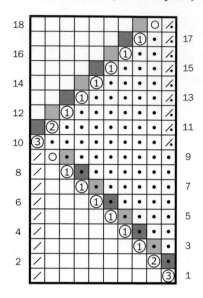

CHART KEY

☐	k1 (RS), p1 (WS)
•	p1 (RS), k1 (WS)
╱	k2tog (RS), p2tog (WS)
╱.	p2tog (RS), k2tog (WS)
○	yo
①	yo with 1 bead
②	yo with 2 beads
③	yo with 3 beads
▨	bead to back (see notes)
▩	bead to front (see notes)

ABBREVIATIONS

k—knit

k1f&b—knit into the front and back of the same stitch

k2tog—knit 2 stitches together

k3tog—knit 3 stitches together

m1L—make one left (with left-hand needle tip lift strand between needles from front to back, k lifted loop through the back)

m1R—make one right (with left-hand needle tip, lift strand between needles from back to front, k lifted loop through the front)

p—purl

p1f&b—purl into the front and back of the same stitch

pm—place marker

psso—pass slipped stitch over

p2tog—purl 2 stitches together

rep—repeat

RS—right side

sl—slip (below)

sl1k2togpo—sl1 knitwise, k2tog, pass slipped stitch over

ssk—slip next 2 sts, one by one, as if to knit; insert tip of left-hand needle from left to right into the fronts of these two slipped stitches and knit them together

s2kpo—slip 2 together knitwise, k1, pass 2 slipped stitches over

st(s) —stitch(es)

tbl—through the back loop

W&T—wrap and turn

WS—wrong side

yo—yarn over

KNITTING ESSENTIALS

▶ Look for this icon throughout the book. Wherever you see it, you'll find a video for the technique on my website: www.nelkindesigns.com.

Basic Techniques

tbl (Through the Back Loop)
Knit tbl

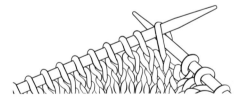

Purl tbl

Typically the right leg of a stitch is to the front of the needle and the left leg is to the back. If instructed to work a stitch through the back loop, work into the left leg of the stitch. This will twist the stitch.

sl (Slipping Stitches)
The pattern will specify which way to slip a stitch. Generally, if there is no instruction, slip the stitch purlwise, which moves the stitch to the other needle without it twisting. If a slipped stitch is part of a decrease, it is slipped knitwise, causing it to lie flat when it is passed over the next stitch worked.

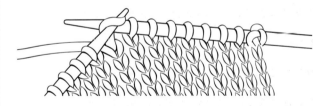

Knitwise: Insert the tip of the right-hand needle into the next stitch on the left-hand needle from left to right (as if you were going to knit it), slip this stitch off the left-hand needle and onto the right-hand one.

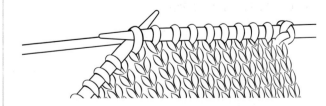

Purlwise: Insert the tip of the right-hand needle into the next stitch on the left-hand needle from right to left (as if you were going to purl it), slip this stitch off the left-hand needle and onto the right-hand one.

Increases

m1R (Make 1 Right)

With the left-hand needle tip lift a strand between the needles from back to front, knit the lifted loop through the front. This creates a right-leaning increase.

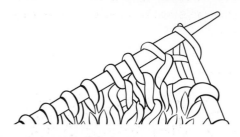

m1L (Make 1 Left)

With left-hand needle tip lift a strand between the needles from front to back, knit the lifted loop through the back. This creates a left-leaning increase.

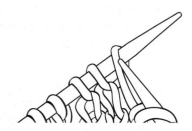

k1f&b (Knit into the Front and Back of a Stitch)

Knit into the front (or right leg) of the stitch as usual and then, before slipping it off the left-hand needle, knit a second stitch through the back (or left leg) as well. This turns one stitch into two.

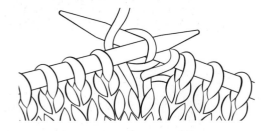

p1f&b (Purl into the Front and Back of a Stitch)

Purl into the front (or right leg) of the stitch as usual and then, before slipping it off the left-hand needle, purl a second stitch through the back (or left leg) as well. This turns one stitch into two.

yo (Yarn Over)

Wrap the yarn around the right-hand needle to make a new stitch with the right leg to the front of the needle, and the left leg to the back. In some situations, a yarn over is worked slightly differently, depending on how it relates to knit and purl stitches on each side of it (page 47).

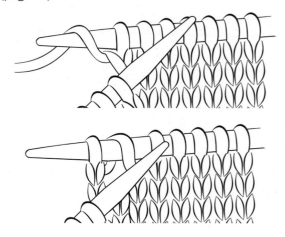

Decreases

k2tog (Knit 2 Together)

With yarn to the back of the work, insert the right-hand needle into the next two stitches on the left-hand needle knitwise, then knit them together. This creates a right-leaning decrease.

k3tog (Knit 3 Together)

With yarn to the back of the work, insert the right-hand needle into the next three stitches on the left-hand needle knitwise, then knit them together. This creates a right-leaning double decrease.

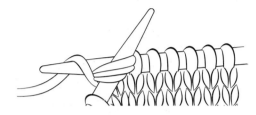

k2togtbl (Knit 2 Together Through the Back Loop)

With yarn to the back of the work, insert the right-hand needle into the back legs of the next two stitches on the left-handed needle knitwise, then knit them together. This creates a left-leaning decrease.

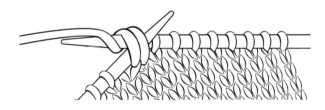

p2tog (Purl 2 Together)

With yarn to the front of the work, insert the right-hand needle into the next two stitches on the left-hand needle purlwise, then purl them together. This creates a right-leaning decrease.

p3tog (Purl 3 Together)

With yarn to the front of the work, insert the right-hand needle into the next three stitches on the left-hand needle purlwise, then purl them together. This creates a right-leaning double decrease.

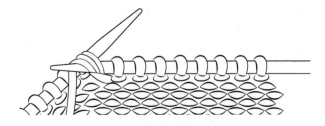

p2togtbl (Purl 2 Together Through the Back Loop)

With yarn to the front of the work, insert the right-hand needle through the back loop of the next two stitches on the left-hand needle purlwise, starting with the stitch farthest away from the end of the needle, then purl them together. This creates a left-leaning decrease.

ssk (Slip, Slip Knit)

Slip the first stitch on the left-hand needle knitwise, slip the second stitch purlwise; insert the tip of the left-hand needle from left to right into the fronts of these two slipped stitches and knit them together. This creates a left-leaning decrease.

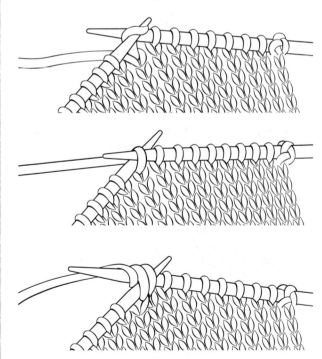

s2kpo (Slip 2, Knit 1, Pass Slipped Stitches Over)

Slip two stitches together knitwise from the left-hand needle onto the right-hand needle, knit the next stitch, and then pass the slipped stitches over the new stitch just made. This creates a centered double decrease.

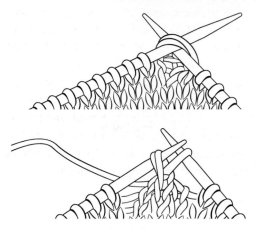

sl1k2togpo (Slip 1, Knit 2 Together, Pass Slipped Stitch Over)

Slip the first stitch on the left-hand needle knitwise onto the right-hand needle, knit the next two stitches together, and then pass the slipped stitch over the new stitch just made on the right-hand needle. This creates a left-leaning double decrease.

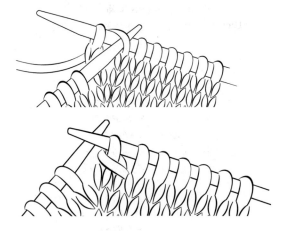

Tricksy Techniques

W&T (Wrap and Turn)

On Right Side: Bring yarn to the front of the work, slip the next stitch purlwise onto the right-hand needle, bring yarn to the back of the work, then slip stitch back to the left-hand needle. Turn work.

On Wrong Side: Bring yarn to the back of the work, slip the next stitch purlwise onto the right-hand needle, bring yarn to the front of the work, then slip stitch back to the left-hand needle. Turn work.

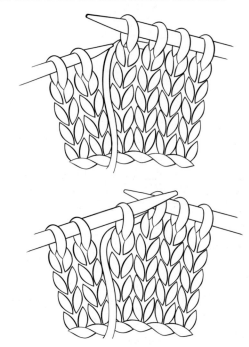

Working Stitches Together with Their Wraps

On Right Side: Insert right needle into the wrap from underneath, and knit the wrap together with the stitch.

On Wrong Side: Insert right needle from underneath into the wrap on the right side (i.e., the side facing away from you); lift it up onto the left-hand needle, and purl it together with the wrapped stitch.

I-Cord

With a double-pointed needle, knit the number of stitches the pattern calls for, and slide the stitches to the other end of the needle. *Do not turn work.* Bringing yarn around the back of the work, begin the next row as before. In a few rows the stitches will tighten up, creating a cord!

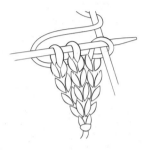

Magic Loop

Magic Loop is worked with a long circular needle in lieu of a shorter circular needle or double-pointed needles. Split the stitches so that half of them are on the front needle, and half on the back, with the extra needle cord creating a loop on the left-hand side of the work. Pull the back needle out with the right hand, which will "shorten" the loop on the left-hand side and allow you to work onto the right-hand needle. Continue across all the stitches on the left-hand needle. Turn the work, pushing the front needle back to make the loop at the left-hand side of the work longer, and then pull out the back needle to begin again. It will help to mark the beginning of the work.

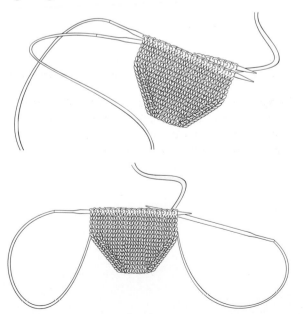

Russian Join

Use this technique for joining a new ball or skein. Keep in mind that it only works with wool and wool blends, and that it won't work with prestrung beads, since they won't be able to slide over the join. (In that case you will simply have to weave in a few ends.) Thread the yarn tail onto a sharp needle. Leaving a 1–2-inch (2.5–5cm) loop, thread that needle back through the yarn, weaving it in and out of the strands of fiber and splitting them as much as possible. Pull the tail of the yarn through, removing the needle, and leaving the loop intact. Thread the new yarn onto the needle and bring it through the loop. Weave that end as you did with the first strand of yarn. Now, it's time for the magic. Gently pull on both ends of the yarn. The loops will tighten up, creating a solid join. Trim ends.

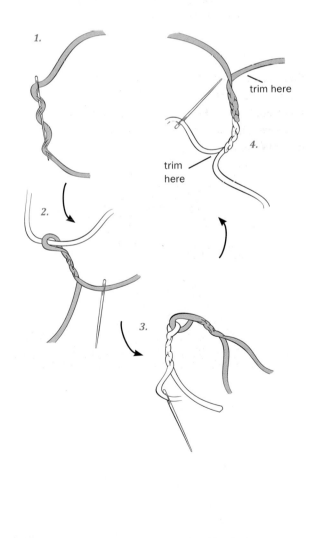

Removing the Provisional Cast-On

Ripping out your provisional cast-on (page 139) is easy! It's easier, though, if you use a smooth yarn that doesn't cling to the working yarn. Just slip the tail with the knot through the last chain made and begin to unzip the chain, picking up the live stitches with a needle that is a size or two smaller than your working needle. Remember to transfer these stitches to your working needle before you begin to work with them.

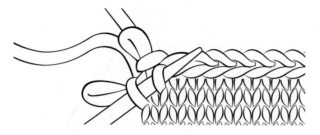

Kitchener Stitch

Hold needles parallel to each other with wrong sides together. Thread the yarn tail onto a tapestry needle.

To set up: Insert the tapestry needle into the first stitch on the *front* needle as if to *purl,* and pull yarn through. Insert the tapestry needle into the first stitch on the *back* needle as if to *knit,* and pull yarn through.

Start grafting: (1) Go into the first stitch on the *front* needle as if to *knit,* pull yarn through, and drop stitch *off* the needle. (2) Go into the next stitch on the front needle as if to *purl,* pull yarn through, and leave stitch *on* the needle. (3) Go into the first stitch on the *back* needle as if to *purl,* pull yarn through, and drop stitch *off* the needle (4) Go into next stitch on the *back* needle as if to *knit,* pull yarn through, and leave stitch *on* the needle. Follow these 4 steps until all stitches have been grafted.

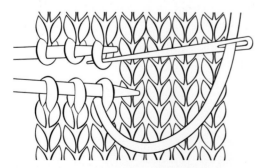

Cast-On Techniques

Long-Tail Cast-On

With a long tail make a slip knot onto the needle. To make your tail long enough, loosely wrap the yarn around your needle 10 times and measure how much yarn is used. Then "do the math" to determine how long your tail should be in relation to the cast-on sts. I always add another bit for "just in case."

With the needle in your right hand, hug both tails with the bottom three fingers of your left hand. Then with your thumb and index finger split these two tails, wrapping one tail around each finger as shown, creating a V. Bring the needle up through the loop on the thumb, and then catch the first strand around the index finger and go back through the loop on the thumb. Release the loop on thumb, tightening up the new stitch, and bring the yarns back to their V formation to begin the next stitch.

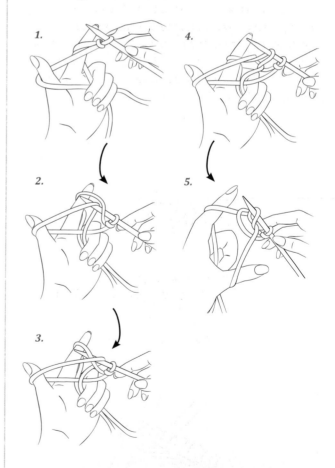

Crochet Cast-On

Place slip knot onto crochet hook in the right hand. With the needle in your left hand, bring the working yarn underneath the needle and then hook the yarn around the crochet hook. Pull this loop through the stitch on the hook. Then bring the yarn between the hook and needle so that it is underneath the needle ready to work the next stitch as before. If worked with scrap yarn, this cast-on is used for the patterns that call for a provisional cast-on.

Knitted-On or Lace Cast-On

▶ Place a slip knot on the left-hand needle. Insert the right-hand needle into the slip knot and knit a stitch. Place this knitted stitch back onto the left-hand needle, being careful not to twist it. Continue knitting a new stitch into the stitch just made until you have the number of stitches the pattern calls for.

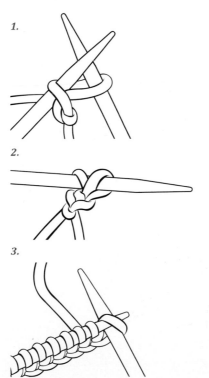

1.

2.

3.

Backwards Loop Cast-On

▶ Place a slip knot on the right-hand needle. With the left hand, wrap yarn so that the working yarn comes behind the right-hand needle, creating a new stitch with a half-hitch knot. Continue until you have the number of stitches the pattern calls for.

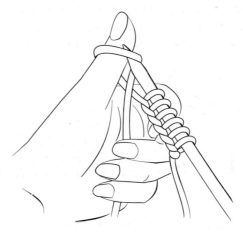

Circular Cast-On

▶ Make a loose overhand knot leaving a 3-inch (7.5cm) tail hanging down the right side. With working yarn, yarn over the right-hand needle. Then reach inside the circle with the right-hand needle and yarn over needle again, pulling the new stitch through. Repeat these last two steps until you have the required number of stitches on the needle. Pull down on the tail, which will magically create the circle.

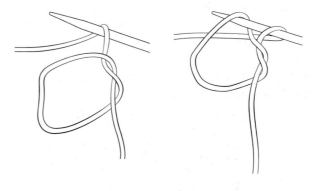

Bind-Off Techniques

Regular Bind-Off

Knit 1 stitch, *knit 1 stitch, then insert the left-hand needle into the front of the second stitch on the right-hand needle. Lift it up and over the first stitch. Repeat from * until all stitches are bound off.

Note: If the pattern calls for binding off in pattern, just knit the knits and purl the purls as they present themselves.

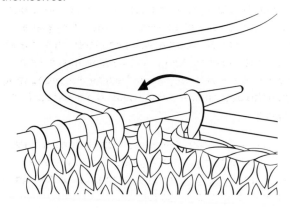

Lace or Elastic Bind-Off

▶ Knit 2 stitches. Insert the left-hand needle into the front of the two stitches on the right-hand needle, knit them together. *Knit 1 stitch (you will now have 2 stitches on right-hand needle), insert the left-hand needle into the front of the 2 stitches on the right-hand needle, knit them together; repeat from * across. Cut yarn and pull through last stitch.

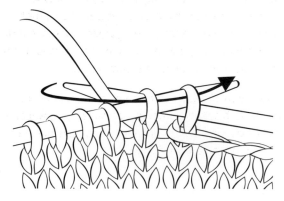

Lace or Elastic Bind-Off in Pattern

Work the first stitch in pattern (i.e., knit a knit stitch, purl a purl stitch).

If the next stitch is a knit stitch: K1, then insert the left-hand needle into the front of the two stitches on the right-hand needle, knit them together.

If the second stitch is a purl stitch: P1, then insert the left-hand needle into the back of the two stitches on the right-hand needle, purl them together.

Work the next stitch in pattern and repeat as established until all stitches are bound off.

Three-Needle Bind-Off

Hold needles parallel to each other with right sides together. *With spare needle go through the first stitch on the front needle *and* the first stitch on the back needle, then knit them together; repeat from * once more. Insert the left-hand needle into the front of the second stitch on the right-hand needle. Lift it up and over the first stitch; continue as established until all stitches are bound off.

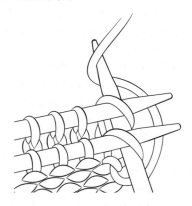

BLOCKING

Blocking transforms your stitches into uniform rows of texture and pattern. Typically, while you are knitting something it will appear to be a blob, a mere shadow of its future blocked self! In my lace classes I like to remind students that lace, in particular, looks like crap until you block it. I find that when I am knitting an intricate piece, I'll constantly be smoothing it out on my leg or the table so I can open up the stitches and see what it "really" looks like.

The simple directions below will help you explore the art of blocking. I refer to it as the "art" of blocking because one shawl can be blocked a multitude of ways. I never realized how true this was until a Mystery Knit-Along I ran in which I counted ten unique, gorgeous ways the shawl had been blocked. (Remember: No one had seen a photo of the finished piece.) Luckily, if you don't like your blocking the first time, or just want to try another way, you can rewet the piece and do it again!

How to Wet-block

Fill a clean sink with warm water (not hot or cold, to avoid shocking the fibers) and a bit of wool soak. There are many products on the market for soaking yarn, such as Soak and Euclan, which are meant to be used as a conditioner and not rinsed out. Don't use a detergent, which will strip the fiber. Let it soak for a good ten or fifteen minutes, or even longer.

Then drain the sink and lift the project up with both hands from underneath—not by one end. Gently squeeze out as much excess water as you can. Lay it flat on a towel or two. Some yarns do bleed a bit of dye, so don't use a pristine white towel! Roll this towel up with the project in it and squeeze out some more of the moisture. For flat items, find a surface you can pin into, away from pets. My cat (the stinker!), *loves* wet wool. It's as if she wants to snuggle with a wet sheep! You can use blocking mats, rubber floor tiles from the hardware store, or a mattress. Be sure to have the measurements or schematics from the pattern close at hand. You'll also need a few materials: rustproof pins, a yardstick and/or ruler, measuring tape, and blocking wires *or* strong buttonhole thread and a needle. If you decide to invest in blocking wires, find a flexible set, like those from Inspinknitty. They have tips that are gentle on fibers and will last a lifetime.

Lay the project down and begin to smooth it into shape. I typically start with pins to hold it down flat to its measurements. Most lace pieces that need to be pulled taut to open up the stitches will benefit from using blocking wires. Just feed the wire in and out along the edge. If you have shaping at the bottom, you can run a wire or pin it out. Keep in mind that everywhere you place a pin it will "pull" out on the fabric, potentially creating a point. Sometimes these points are just what you want (as in the Fornido Shawlette, page 57); other times you want a straight edge (as in the Trapeze Scarf, page 121).

If you don't have wires, you can use strong buttonhole thread. This is a more time-consuming technique but works almost as well as wires. Thread a long piece of buttonhole thread on a needle, and then run it in and out along the edge. Wrap the thread around a T-pin stuck into the blocking board. Holding the thread taut, wrap the other end around a second pin and stick it in place.

For three-dimensional shapes, such as tams or hats, lay them flat to dry, or roll up rags or a towel to use as a head form. For tams, use a small plate that fits inside it to help form the top.

How to Steam-Block

Some items, such as the Bulb Cuff and Necklace (page 95), are small enough that you can steam-block them instead of wet-blocking them. The trick to steam-blocking is to place a towel between the work and the iron so you don't damage the yarn. Spritz the piece with water to dampen it, lay down the towel, and then run a *hot* iron over it. Typically items that are steam-blocked aren't ever washed, as their shape and size can change with wet-blocking, so keep this in mind should you choose to steam-block.

In the scope of this book it wasn't possible to show you how to block every design, so consult my website for photos and readers' projects if you have questions on how to block a specific piece.

RESOURCES

YARN

Blue Sky Alpacas
www.blueskyalpacas.com

The Brown Sheep Co., Inc.
www.brownsheep.com

Classic Elite Yarns
www.classiceliteyarns.com

Elsebeth Lavold
www.knittingfever.com/c/
elsebeth-lavold/yarn/

The Fibre Company/Kelbourne
Woolens
www.thefibreco.com

Galler Yarns
www.galleryarns.com

Jill Draper Makes Stuff
www.jilldraper.com

Knitted Wit
www.knittedwit.com

Knit Whits/Freia Fibers
www.freiafibers.com

Koigu
www.koigu.com

Lion Brand Yarn
www.lionbrand.com

Lorna's Laces
www.lornaslaces.net

Madelinetosh
www.madelinetosh.com

Manos Del Uruguay/Fairmount
Fibers
www.fairmountfibers.com

Noro
www.knittingfever.com/c/noro/
yarn/

Prism Yarns
www.prismyarn.com

Stonehedge Fiber Mill
www.stonehedgefibermill.com

Shibui Knits
www.shibuiknits.com

Space Cadet Creations
www.spacecadetcreations.com

Swans Island Company
www.swansislandcompany.com/
catalog/yarn

Sweet Georgia Yarns
www.sweetgeorgiayarns.com

BEADS, BUTTONS, AND CLASPS

Nelkin Designs (US)
www.nelkindesigns.com/kits

Art Beads (US)
www.artbeads.com

Beads Direct (UK)
www.beadsdirect.co.uk

Caravan Beads (US)
www.caravanbeads.com

Cranberry (Australia)
http://www.cranberry.net.au/

Fire Mountain Gems (US)
www.firemountaingems.com

Fusion Beads (US)
www.fusionbeads.com

GJ Beads (UK)
www.gjbeads.co.uk

Glitzer Perlen (Germany)
www.glitzerperlen.de

Jilly Beads (UK)
www.jillybeads.co.uk

Land of Odds (US)
www.landofodds.com

Lima Beads (US)
www.limabeads.com

Melissa Jean Designs (US)
www.melissajean.net

Miyuki Perlen (Germany)
www.miyukiperlen.de

SeedBeading (Australia)
www.seedbeading.com.au

The Beading Room (Canada)
www.thebeadingroom.com

BOOKS

JC Briar, *Chart Reading Made
Simple*
www.jcbriar.com

Miriam Felton, *Twist and Knit*
www.mimknits.com

Bev Galeskas, *The Magic Loop*

June Hemmons Hiatt, *The
Principles of Knitting*

Clara Parkes, *The Knitter's Book
of Yarn*

WITH GRATITUDE

Without the eagle eyes of my tech editor, Kate Atherley, this book would be a mere shadow of itself. Over the course of the last few years, Kate has helped shape the pattern writer I have become through her fervent understanding of how the knitter's mind works. Also, she has mad math skills, and I like to make her brain hurt! Thanks, Kate!

A huge thank-you to the many generous yarn companies and hand-dyers who have supported my obsession by providing me with the necessary tool of my trade—YARN!

Dear pattern testers, y'all put some incredible energy and brainpower into knitting *all* the patterns in this book and helping me make them better than ever! Thanks to Ana Cecilia F., Brenda W., Cathy A., Cathy M., Colleen, Cynthia W., Debbie D., Elizabeth M., Heather C., Jan H., Jeane M., Justine, Karen S. C., Kelly P., Kristin C., Lorrie H., Mary M., Susan M., and Susan S.

An extra-special shout-out must be made to Colleen, Justine, Ana Cecilia, and Lorrie, who never ever ever said no to me when a pattern needed them and always came back with the most useful, thoughtful, and encouraging feedback. Seriously, this book wouldn't have happened without you! And to Ava, who kept my kit business running smoothly while the book was in progress!

I was lucky and honored to be chosen by Potter Craft to work on this book. Their enthusiasm, endless amounts of energy, and expertise helped make this book more beautiful and complex than I imagined. I am thrilled to have worked with you all! A special thank-you must be expressed to Caitlin Harpin, my editor, who really "got" what I was creating and made it work!

The book's photo shoot with Lauren Volo and team at the Angevine Tree Farm is a treasured memory. Who knew shooting twenty-five pieces in two days could be so *fun!* Also, thanks to Jill Swenson at Swenson Book Development for providing me with sound and timely contractual, business, and authorly advice!

A debt of gratitude must be paid to my parents, who always supported my passions without fail.

To my people: You know who you are, and I don't know what I would do without you! Thanks for listening to my yammering about this book and more, even when you had no idea what I was talking about! I am blessed to have all of you in my life.

Oh, Max and Bella, thanks for patiently waiting while I knit just one more row. LOVE YOU!

INDEX